Mind The Gap:

A Guide To Gap Years From Someone Who's Survived One

Abby Trombley

First Print-On-Demand Edition

Produced and Distributed By the Author in Association with:

Library Partners Press
ZSR Library
Wake Forest University
1834 Wake Forest Road
Winston-Salem, North Carolina 27106

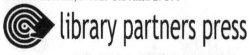

www.librarypartnerspress.org

ACKNOWLEDGMENTS

I would like to thank:

the people at Lake Research Partners for teaching and challenging me,

the country of South Africa for amazing me and my "Bush House family" for sharing it with me,

my professors and classmates at the London School of Economics for inspiring me, and

and my family for supporting me through it all.

CONTENTS

THE BACKPACK

In the backpack I carried,
the beatings of the past I had buried.
So I took them out,
and packed instead
Curiosity that I watered and fed.

The backpack saw
press ironed clothes,
African mountains,
and animal tails.

It saw
train stations,
monuments,
and red dirt under my nails.

Dragged into the sea of humility
the backpack and me.
The backpack carries my gift and my story,
my burden and my glory.

In my backpack I now carry with me,
who I am,
who I was,
who I want to be.

ONE

Taking the Leap

"There are no wrong turnings. Only paths we had not known we were meant to walk."

— Guy Gavriel Kay

My gap year was born, more or less, out of a failure. When I was in high school I was a dual enrollment student, meaning I took half of my classes at high school and the other half at the University of Vermont. This allowed me to graduate high school a year early. Therefore the first time I applied to colleges it was my junior year and I was sixteen years old. I was ambitious and incredibly naive, and refused to listen to anyone who mentioned the term "safety school." I knew I had the option to take a gap year and retry the process the following year and still be the same age as my classmates, but that didn't prepare me for the result come April: nine rejection letters with my name on them. Dartmouth, Davidson, Middlebury, Williams, Harvard, Duke, Boston College, William and Mary, Vanderbilt.

I wasn't excited about the idea of taking a gap year, although now I know the chance to have an entire year to go anywhere and do anything is the best gift I ever fell into. I was scared, because like I was in high school as a dual-enrollment student, I was going to be on an independent path again. In the moment I desperately wanted the communal experience one has at college, and instead I would spend the entire next year on a solo journey. I was rejected from nine of the top institutions in the country and to say my confidence was shaken is a severe understatement. In addition, I knew my gap year couldn't involve riding horses, which had been my passion for the last ten years of my life.

My entire identity had been built upon my success in school and my love of riding. With those two losses, I didn't know what was left of me. My gap year thrust me into the world to go find it. Even though it was the result of a magnitude of failure I had never experienced before, it ended up being the greatest thing I have ever accomplished.

Firstly, I want to address some of the misconceptions about gap years:

Gap years are a time to float around freely with no responsibilities and it is all just a lot of fun.

Gap years are incredibly hard. They require planning, self initiative, and independence. You are not following a tried path. There is no academic advisor guiding you in what to do, there is no R.A. checking up on you along the way. You won't

4

have a group of peers to compare and relate to. Most of all, it requires a lot of bravery to choose the less traveled path. But there is an element to that belief that is true; gap years are a lot of fun because you will have incredibly unique experiences. In my gap year, I was at a midterm election party with people who had a direct hand in getting candidates elected. I was chased by a lion while on horseback in South Africa. I swam in the Mediterranean Sea. This is to show all the challenges of a gap year are more than worth it.

Gap years are for people who are lost, have no ambition or drive, and want to slack off.

In my gap year, I have:

- created graphs, presentations and proofed reports for winning midterm election candidates and many national organizations
- removed up to 70 snares in the African bush therefore saving 70 animals' lives- in just one morning (and did this many mornings)
- attended a summer school program at a world-class institution
- earned thousands of dollars at a job
- all at the age of 17

This is just to name a few. I'd say I've been pretty productive.

If you choose to take a gap year you will be "behind" other people who chose to go to college right away.

It is just the opposite. Many of the experiences you have in gap years are ones you would typically have during, or even after, college. For example, most people don't have an internship experience until summers in between college or post-graduating. The three other interns I worked with at Lake Research Partners were all college graduates. You can have an experience living abroad which again is something most people do their sophomore, junior or senior year of college. You might work a job, probably a minimum wage job, at which you will learn things you will probably never learn in the "bubble" that is college. Your gap year experiences will then shape the way you approach and absorb material in the classroom, and give you a unique perspective from your classmates'. In addition, it makes you better prepared for the new opportunities you will be offered at college, because your resume will probably be bigger and more colorful than the ones you are competing against for internships, jobs, research opportunities, etc. Therefore, by taking a gap year you are actually *ahead* of your classmates that have gone straight to college from high school, not behind.

This past year has been the most exciting, most difficult, and most surprising year of my life. I commend you on your choice to take or consider a gap year, as they are not for the faint of heart. At this point in time gap years are fairly unchartered territory, so I hope this guide can help you in filling your blank pages. Start by knowing that to be eighteen years old and having an entire year to do whatever you want is a life-changing opportunity already.

TWO

Planning Your Gap Year
(and why you really can't)

"Then took the other, as just as fair,
And having perhaps the better claim,
Because it was grassy and wanted wear."
- Robert Frost "The Road Not Taken"

To describe my year in short: September through November I went to Washington, D.C. and did an internship at Lake Research Partners (LRP), a political polling and campaign strategy firm. I lived in a women's dorm on Capitol Hill, and worked 9-6 at LRP. During the month of December I worked a holiday season job. January through March I spent in the remote South African bush, volunteering at a game reserve and in the local community. Our main anti-poaching task was to remove snares in the bush that are used to catch and kill wildlife. We also worked on conservation projects, and volunteered at the orphanage in the local community. April through June I returned home and worked at a market and deli. In July, I took a course at the London School of Economics and Political Science summer school.

I didn't really plan my gap year ahead of time, I made decisions as I went along. By early July of 2014 my plans to go to D.C. were finalized, and I expected to be there until Thanksgiving. After that I didn't know where I would go or what I would do. In late November I was sitting in my dorm room in D.C. On a Google search I found the program The Leap, with whom I went to South Africa. Before that moment, I had no interest in going abroad as the idea of it terrified me. In the past my mother had shown me one study abroad program after another and I rejected every one of them. But after reading the description of The Leap's program in South Africa, I emailed the program director in the UK before even telling my parents about it.

It was a volunteer program focused on anti-poaching and wildlife conservation and it involved riding horses every day. I knew immediately this was what I was going to do. I was officially signed up for the program less than four weeks before I got on a plane to Johannesburg. Ten weeks later I returned home and again, had no plans for what I would do until I went to Wake Forest in the fall. A week later I found a job at a local market/deli, which was a tough adjustment from the thrill of living in South Africa. But rattling around my brain was my friend's (who has also taken a gap year) strong recommendation of the London School of Economics summer school program. I set to work in figuring out how to make that possible, and eventually the third and final portion of my gap year was planned.

Please note: I don't mean to make it sound like organizing these different programs is easy. The next section is about how to fund your gap year, which was one of the biggest challenges I faced. Every time I chose to partake in one of these experiences, I had to figure out how we would fund it. It is fun to research and choose a program, because there are so many fascinating, thrilling and unique experiences you can have in a gap year. But the hard part is figuring out how to make it work. That is why I would recommend planning your gap year in entirety before the year starts, if you can. That way you can have a budget, and plan how you are going to spend and earn your money.

However, right after graduating I wasn't in a place where I could plan my entire year ahead of time. I was so overwhelmed I could only think what was right in front of me, and at the time that was D.C. Like I said, before I started my gap year I never wanted to go abroad and therefore could not have chosen to do that any sooner. I needed my experience in D.C. to show me how capable I was, which gave me the confidence to go abroad. Every experience you have will make your world bigger, which will grow your desire to see and accomplish more. Once I was in South Africa, I made friends with kids my age who lived all over Europe, which spurred me to want to spend the next portion of my gap year in London.

Therefore I needed my internship in D.C. to be able to go to South Africa, and I needed my time in South Africa to find the desire to go to London. My personal growth with each experience showed me I could do more and that I wanted more.

I surprised myself often over the course of my gap year, but I will tell you ahead of time; you will change during your gap year, probably a lot. Your capabilities, opinions, knowledge, and aspirations will all change. Your beliefs will be challenged, your habits will transform, and you will discover what truly matters to you and what does not. You will find you can do so much more than what you thought you could. Therefore, it might not be possible to plan the entire year ahead of time, because it will surprise you.

That being said, this will be the first time in your life that there are no set expectations, and so you might want structure. Before this, every year was predetermined; you had freshman year of high school, you took the SATs junior year, applied to colleges senior year. Now, the pages are blank for you to fill, and that is really daunting. In addition, there is a lot of pressure to make your time meaningful. Therefore my suggestion is this: while you are being responsible and sensibly planning, take advantage of the freedom of a gap year and start by picking something that draws your interest. That might be a country you have always wanted to visit, exploring a job you might want to have one day, or even a lifestyle that you have always wanted to try. Then, figure out how you are going to make it possible- how you are going to fund it.

There are companies specifically designed to help you plan your gap year. I didn't use one of these services, but I know people who did and found it helpful. This is particularly helpful if you plan to go abroad, and want to find out information about a program that is not based in the U.S. Programs that take students abroad vary greatly in how well they are run, and a gap year planning company will be able to tell you which are better than others. It is also beneficial if you are not accepted to a college yet, and want to know how to structure your gap year to best represent you in the application process. Below is a list of several consulting companies that offer this service.

- Center for Interim Programs
    o Based in Princeton, NJ and Northampton, MA
    o Cost: $2,550
    o Contact: 609.683.4300
- Taking Off
    o Based in Amherst, NH
    o Cost: $2,100
    o Contact: 781.545.8231
- En Route Consulting
    o Based in Stowe, VT
    o Cost: $950-$1,500
    o Contact: 609.529.1459

- Taylor the Gap
  - Based in Boulder/Denver, CO
  - Cost: $475-$750
  - Contact: 303.588.2630
- Gap Year Design
  - Based in Los Angeles, CA
  - Cost: $1,650
  - Contact: gapyeardesign@gmail.com
- Gap Year Explorer
  - Based in Washington, D.C.
  - Cost: $300-$500
  - Contact: 703.732.7524

As you can see, these services are expensive and you might not want or need to spend that money when you could be spending it on the experience you want to have. I believe that as long as you know what is meaningful to you, you will be able to plan a gap year on your own. The programs you choose might not be "guaranteed" to be exactly like they say they are, but by taking a gap year you are taking a huge leap of faith anyways. My program in South Africa turned out to be very different than I expected it to be. I had a lot of fun anyways, and learning how to accept and adapt to unexpected situations are great skills to have in life.

The first two weeks I spent in South Africa I was disappointed. We weren't spending as much time doing the volunteer work as I thought we would, the leadership was much more relaxed than I expected, and we had more free time than I wanted. After the first two weeks I decided I needed to give myself a serious attitude adjustment. I realized that even though we weren't "making a difference" at the level I wanted to, I was in this amazing country where I was seeing and experiencing incredible things every day. I didn't have to be removing invasive species for four hours a day; I was being imprinted every time we galloped past a herd of zebra, looked into a lion's eyes, or even just sweat under the sun that possesses unmatchable power in that hemisphere. The world I knew was changing, and that itself was enough.

I remember one night in South Africa, myself and two other girls were pressed up against the bathroom's floor-to-ceiling window. We were watching three elephants that had wandered into the yard and were lingering no more than seven feet away from us. The larger female elephant turned around so that she was facing us. Her ears flopped back and forth as she made small movements with her trunk. For a while she just stood there. We had turned off all the lights in the room so only a flashlight illuminated her presence. Around me was a chorus of "Wow!" and "This is awesome" but I couldn't think of any words that would justify her magnificence. I didn't want to ever leave this trance that the elephant and I were locked in; in the moment it felt like a sacred interaction. It felt out of this world- in my normal world elephants showed up behind bars in a zoo or in Animal Planet episodes, but here I was with her right in front of me.

My point is that even if you use a professional consultant to map out your year, or spend hours yourself pouring over websites and reviews, you will never be able to completely plan your gap year. That moment with the elephants was not in any itinerary and I couldn't have paid a consultant to construct it. Your experiences will throw things at you that you didn't expect, but you will be most surprised by the change that occurs within you. It will not turn out exactly the way you expected, and that is a good thing.

The main types of experiences people have in gap years are:

Internships

There are so many types of internships you can have and the situations vary greatly. Sometimes, certain companies or organizations have internship programs that are already designed and running. This is often the case with government organizations. Even within these programs, there is variation in what you will be doing. For example, I have a friend who did an internship for the State of Vermont. This means she worked in the governor of Vermont's office. Her main job was in correspondence; she read letters sent to the governor and sent replies. If you are interested in working in public policy, government institutions have a plethora of internship opportunities that range from your local office to Capitol Hill. My internship was also in politics, but it was with a company, as opposed to a government office. It also had a formal "internship program," and I worked with three other interns. My main job was to proof the reports written by the analysts. This means I would be checking their work for small grammatical mistakes or errors in numbers before the material was sent to a client.

I expected that as an intern my work would be pretty basic- filing, data entry, answering phone calls, even going on coffee runs. While I did end up doing all of these things, most of my time was spent doing substantive work. I had a lot of responsibility with no room for error, and was expected to complete this work in an incredibly fast-paced and high-pressure environment (it was election season after all). But this meant I got to do interesting work for well-known clients, and learned so much. At the same time, I spent some days doing data entry for eight straight hours. Therefore expect to do the grunt work, but also be prepared to be depended on and to add value.

While some internship programs are expansive and well-established, don't count out local professionals, or smaller businesses and organizations. If there is something you are drawn to, I wouldn't hesitate to contact the person you want to learn from. You might be able to exchange work you can offer for the knowledge and experience you will get from it. While I was in high school, I was able to shadow an orthopedic surgeon in the emergency department by simply reaching out to a family friend who is a surgical resident. Work your connections, and never be afraid to ask.

There are so many benefits to doing an internship, the main one being it is a great thing for your resume. Like I said before, most people don't have an internship until mid-college or post-college, so you will have an advantage when applying for later opportunities already having experience and references. I cannot describe how much you will learn every single day. From my internship at Lake Research Partners I learned so much about political polling, but also gained other skills that are applicable to many environments such as office skills, how to interact with superiors, how to interact with clients, how to manage your work load, how to manage time, and much more. Lastly, you will make connections with already-established professionals in the field you might work in one day. Celinda Lake, the owner and president of the firm I interned at, is one of the most prominent pollsters in America. The fact that she even knows my name is invaluable.

Unfortunately the majority of internships (especially for people who have only graduated high school) are unpaid. Some, like my internship, offer a stipend. A stipend is monetary compensation, but is smaller than an actual paycheck. The other difficulty with internships is that they do not provide housing.

You might be able to find an internship in the area you live in and therefore could live at home, but if not you are going to have to find an affordable place to live. When I was in D.C. I lived in Thompson Markward Hall (see below), which is dormitory-style housing specifically for young women doing internships or working in D.C. short term. This was an affordable place to live that offered breakfast and dinner each day and security twenty-four hours a day in a city. This was a really great option, and without it I probably wouldn't have been able to move to D.C. on my own at age seventeen. Listed below are several other establishments in various cities that offer similar situations. Most of these are apartment-style (Thompson Markward is pretty unique in how it runs like a college dorm), so if that kind of situation isn't for you you'll have to pick an internship in a location where you can live with family or friends.

- Thompson Markward Hall
    - Washington, D.C. (located on Capitol Hill)
    - Girls only
    - Dormitory-style rooms, hal,l bathrooms, 24/7 security, breakfast and dinner Monday-Saturday, breakfast Sunday
    - $1040 per month
    - www.tmhdc.org
- WISH (Washington Intern Student Housing)
    - Washington, D.C. (located on Capitol Hill and Woodley Park)
    - Houses only interns, shared and private roos available, town home or apartment style
    - Rates vary by apartment style and time of year
    - www.internsdc.com

- NYC Intern
  - New York City, New York (several locations)
  - Furnished apartments, 24/7 security
  - Rates vary by location, type of apartment, and time of year
  - www.nycintern.org
- University Center's Chicago Summer Housing
  - Chicago, IL
  - Furnished apartments, meal plans
  - Rates vary by type of room and dates of stay
  - www.chicagosummerhousing.com
- Zuma Housing Westwood
  - Los Angeles, CA
  - Affordable apartments in several locations
  - Rates vary by apartment
  - www.zoomahousing.com

The best advice I can give for picking an internship is to find one that has many other interns. The hardest part about my time in D.C. was that I was lonely. The other interns I worked with were college graduates, so they were at a very different place in their lives than I was. While I did make several great friends, I didn't have a peer group I belonged in. It's hard enough to be working at a challenging internship, and living in a city by yourself, you don't want to be doing it on your own. If you can find an internship that has a large group of interns that are in a similar situation to you that will make a huge difference. Even though they probably won't all be gap year students, if there is a large group and it is a well-established program there is a better chance you will find a group of people you can connect to.

Travel Abroad

There are many different ways to spend time abroad during your gap year. You can do a study abroad program, meaning you take classes at a local university. There are even programs where you can repeat your senior year in a different country. You can also go abroad to volunteer, like I did. You can go abroad to pursue a certain passion, like the art program my friend Amy did in Italy in Greece. There are outdoor adventure type programs, where you spend your time backpacking, traveling by kayak, rock climbing, back country skiing, etc. There are even some programs designed purely for travel and exploring new places. The options are limitless and there are many, many programs out there. I would recommend going abroad with a program as opposed to planning a trip on your own. That way all the details that are tricky to figure out, especially if you are going somewhere remote (i.e. housing, travel plans, etc.), will already be taken care of. Most importantly, traveling with a program will provide a group of peers to share your experience with and a leader to guide you.

This was the greatest difference between my time in D.C. and in South Africa; while in D.C. I was completely on my own, in South Africa I belonged to a group of fifteen other people my age with whom I spent every second of the day with.

Being with the same group of people to eat meals, relax, and complete every activity with has a powerful effect, especially being in the remote South African bush where we didn't see many other people. You are all having these incredible experiences and facing trials that all come with living abroad, and doing this together causes you to become close to and dependent on one another. Also, I was one of only two Americans in my group. Most of the kids were from England, so I felt like I was exposed to two cultures during my time there: South African and British culture. I got to really understand a whole other perspective, and now I have connections around the globe, making my world that much bigger and better. This is something you don't want to miss out on- so go with a group of people your age, preferably people you didn't know beforehand.

You can go abroad for an entire year, for a semester, or less time than that. Housing varies by program; sometimes you will be living with a host family, other times the program will provide a house like mine did. While living with a host family might seem a little scary, it is the best way to be fully immersed in the country. That being said, separate housing might be better in a country where safety is a concern. Most programs will take this into account when they choose accommodation, but it is a good thing to keep in mind when you are doing your research. I didn't feel like I was missing out at all by living in our own housing. At Bush House, where we lived, we ate traditional South African food, often experienced power and running water outages, and frequently removed prehistoric-looking bugs and other critters from our rooms. The house was completely open to the bush; we had a family of wildebeest that took up residence in our backyard, and sometimes we would be eating dinner outside and have to run in the house quickly because a herd of wild elephants would be walking through the yard. This way you are living somewhere that is safe, but are still experiencing the country firsthand. If you are looking to live on the edge a little, don't worry either; the most common snake at Bush House was a Mozambique spitting cobra, one of the most dangerous snakes in the world. I still felt like we had plenty of adventure.

You can begin researching travel abroad programs two ways: starting with a country you want to go to, or with what you want to do. I didn't initially think I wanted to go to South Africa; I researched programs that involved riding horses and that is how I found my program. But if you know there is a certain place you want to go, start by researching trips that are based in that country.

Travel abroad programs are expensive. One way to make it possible is to schedule your time abroad later in the year, so you can work at the beginning of the year and save your money. I will describe how I did this more in detail in the next chapter, but most kids in my group had done the same thing.

I cannot possibly list all the travel abroad programs out there because there are so many. Instead I picked three examples of companies with whom I've had personal experience for you to start your research with.

The Leap

- volunteering, with a variety of causes and locations around the world
- 6 or 10 week programs
- This is the program I went to South Africa with. The company itself is communicative, flexible and informative and offers programs in many exciting locations. At the location there wasn't anyone from The Leap itself, it was run by local employees, so I'm sure the programs vary based on where they are located.

Gap 360

- internships, paid work, adventure programs, volunteering
- length varies from 2 weeks to 5 months
- Gap 360 has a program at Kwa Madwala, the game reserve I was on in South Africa, so I interacted with the kids that were with this program. One advantage of this company is that there is a lot of variation in the time length and types of activities you are doing. You can go for 2 or 4 weeks if that is all you want, or you can go for several months during which you will travel to several different location and projects.

Carpe Diem

- travel, volunteering, study abroad

- 3 months or year-long programs
- This is a very well-run program that my friend went to Australia, New Zealand and Fiji with. It is on the pricier side, but it definitely has a clear purpose, good planning and quality leadership.

Because I can't research every single program out there, I put together a list of questions to ask and consider when you're doing your own research.

- How many kids are typically in a group?
- What is the average age of participants?
- Where are most participants from? Is it pretty mixed, or do they tend to come from one region?
- Is the group leader hired by the company, or the local community?
  - If he/she if from the local community, has the company ever met the group leader?
  - If he/she is not from the local community, how much experience does he/she have with the area?
- Is there a language barrier in the country you are going to, and if yes, how will that be managed?
- What type of housing will you be living in?
- Do you need travel insurance or any special type of medical insurance?

- What security measures are in place where you will be living? This is important whether you will be in a first or third world country.

- How much money will you need to bring for personal expenses? Once I week my group in South Africa went to the local town to have a meal and go to the grocery store. All our meals at home were provided for but in town we could buy any snacks we might want throughout the week. There were also a couple "extra" activities we had to pay for, like our trips to Kruger National Park. I also spent money on gifts for people back home. If you are living somewhere less remote, you might go to local restaurants/stores more often. Because the currency exchange rate is different in every country, it's hard for me to estimate how much you will spend each week, so it is definitely something to ask the program about.

- Is there cell service/Wi-Fi where you will be living? Bush House did not have Wi-Fi and that was a really great thing because it meant we actually had to talk to each other. The reason I ask about this is for communicating with your family back home. How easy/difficult will it be able to call/email them? We went to the game reserve's lodge once a week for an hour to use wifi so you could call/Skype your parents and friends then, and that was the perfect amount of time.

- Do you need any special vaccinations before living in that country?
- What will a typical day look like?
- What do you need to pack? Is there anything particular to the program that you need to have?
- How structured is each day? Are weekends "free time?"
    - If they are, what do kids typically do in this time?
- What will the food be like?
    - Is it provided for you each day, are you cooking your own meals?
    - Is it "western-type" food or local cuisine?
    - Are special diets (i.e. vegetarian, vegan) accommodated? (There were two vegetarians in my group who had a very hard time in South Africa, so this is an important one to ask about if it applies to you.)

Another type of travel experience you can have is "backpacking." Some people consider "backpacking" to be trekking through the wilderness carrying everything including a tent on your back. But it can also simply mean traveling to many different places, spending a short amount of time in each place. After studying in London, I backpacked to three different countries in Europe: France, Switzerland, and Italy. Planning a backpacking trip through Europe is super exciting, and a lot more complicated than you might think. Below I broke down the task into four main elements:

Where do you want to go?

I knew that I was starting and ending my travel in London, so I chose to plan my route to be somewhat circular. If you have to start and end your travel in the same place, a circular route makes most sense. There isn't much for me to tell you about this part- it's all about what countries and cities you want to explore! My recommendation is to spend at least two nights in each place. That only gives you one full day there, and that isn't enough time to see everything you want to see, along with adjusting to a new place with a foreign language, foreign transportation system, etc. But if you are on a time crunch (like I was) two nights might be the most you can do.

To find out how long it will take to travel place-to-place (by train) you can use the Eurail Rail Planner app. This allows you to plug in two locations, and it will find trains going that route and tell you how much time they take. However, before I left I read somewhere that if, for example, a train is supposed to take four hours, budget twice that amount of time for travel time. Those four hours do not take into account the time you need to get to the train station, wait for the train, get checked in, wait for the train to depart, get off the train, and then find your next hostel in a new city. That four hour trip has now turned into an eight hour trip, almost an entire day. So keep that in mind when you are planning your travel days.

How are you going to get there?

When most people travel around Europe, they use the Eurail. The Eurail is a system of high-speed trains that go all over the continent. There are several different kinds of passes you can buy and they vary in price.

- Global Pass- you can travel to any country.
- Select Pass- you can travel to four bordering countries.
- Regional Pass- you can travel to two bordering countries.
- One Country Pass- you can travel around one country of your choosing.

Once you select a pass, you can choose how long you need it to be valid for, and how many days of that time period are going to be "travel" days. The prices increase as the number of travel days increase.

Unfortunately, the Eurail does not include travel to/around the U.K. Therefore if you want to travel to/from London (or anywhere else in the U.K.) you have to buy another train ticket on the Eurostar. There is also an option to fly. I found the flight prices to be cheaper than train tickets, so I flew from London to Paris and Paris to London.

The Eurail also offers night trains, so if you need to travel a far distance you can do so at night, sleep on the train, and not lose a day you could be exploring a fantastic city!

Where are you going to stay?

There are several different options for accommodations while you are backpacking. The most common choice that has existed forever is youth hostels. Hostels are like a cheaper, less comfortable version of a hotel. You can stay in a private room, a mixed-gender dorm (bunk beds in one room) or a female-only dorm. My friend and I stayed in private rooms or female-only dorms, depending on which was cheaper for that specific hostel. Hostels range in price from $20/night to $90/night depending on what kind of room you want, what dates you are traveling, and what city you were in. We were able to book all our rooms for between $20/night to $45/night. You must reserve a room/bed ahead of time. During our travels, we met some people that hadn't booked a bed/room ahead of time. This seemed to be really stressful, not knowing where you were going to sleep that night. In addition, it is a lot more expensive last-minute. A lot of hostels also offer free Wi-Fi, lockers, and breakfast. We found all of our hostels through hostelworld.com, a site that has reviews of each hostel and is very easy to use.

Another choice that is increasing in popularity is Airbnb. With Airbnb, you can rent either a single room or an entire apartment from someone for the length of your stay. Sometimes this can be cheaper than a hostel. The website offers reviews of the apartments and the hosts. Sometimes the hosts will be there during your stay and sometimes they won't. From the reviews you can get a sense of the people who own the building will be there, or if this is a second home that they mainly rent out.

My friend and I stayed in an Airbnb when we were in Milan. I was nervous about staying in an apartment with people we didn't know, so we opted to rent a whole apartment. Believe it or not, we were able to rent an apartment for only $46/night, and split between the two of us, this was cheaper than staying in a hostel. Our Airbnb stay turned out to be really nice. We had more space than usual, and best yet we had a washing machine we used ASAP!

One disadvantage with Airbnb is you don't get to meet other backpackers. It was really fun to meet other people in hostels and hear about where they had been, and where they were going. We even met two guys in Interlaken, Switzerland, that we met up with in Nice a few days later when we found out we were going to be there at the same time. Another thing to consider is if there is a language barrier between you and your host. The person that showed us around the apartment the first day only spoke Italian, so needless to say we didn't grasp much she said! Overall though, I was really happy with our Airbnb experience.

What do you need to bring?

Obviously for backpacking in Europe the most important item you need is- a backpack! There are backpacks specifically designed for travel. When I was researching this, I read that one would need a 50L backpack. Because I also had to pack for three weeks in London, I chose a 65L pack. I ordered an Osprey backpack, but there are so many choices out there depending on your style preference. My recommendation is to buy one that zips open like a suitcase-not one that only opens from the top like a hiking backpack. This makes it much easier to find things.

It turns out that my 65L backpack was way too big! It was a little different for me because I had to carry everything I had needed from my previous three weeks in London. But if I had only been backpacking, I could have carried half the amount of clothes. Standing next to other backpackers, my pack looked a bit absurd in it's size. It's weight made it pretty difficult for me to carry it around. I would definitely recommend a 50L backpack.

As for clothing, this obviously depends on the length of your travel and where you are going. But in my experience, traveling for eleven days I believe I only would have needed four-five outfits, and two pairs of shoes (one being sneakers).

Other essentials:

- Lock: for your backpack, or a locker in a hostel
- Travel/camping towel: These are lightweight, quick-drying towels that take up very little space in your bag.
- Travel size toiletries (soap, shampoo, and conditioner): These aren't provided for you like they would be in a hotel.

- Shoes you can wear in the shower- they aren't the cleanest!

- An international phone plan: If you are going abroad for a substantial period of time and staying in whole country that whole time, get a local Sim card. If you are backpacking, get an international phone plan for the period of time you will be traveling. For a small charge each month, you can text and have a small amount of data.

I hope this can help in finding the right travel experience for you. Going abroad will probably be the most exciting thing you've done in your life yet. Wherever you go, you will have incredibly unique experiences.

You will become an expert in problem-solving. You will reach a level of independence not even college will give you. You will form bonds with the people in your group that you will value forever.

You will gain a perspective that will challenge everything you accepted to be true.

You will have moments where you will literally think to yourself, *this is a moment I need to savor, this is a moment I will one day tell my children about.* You will bring home stories that are inspiring, tragic, unbelievable, hilarious.

So be open to and ready for your life to change, and expect the unexpected.

Studying

Some people take a gap year to take a break from schoolwork before they start college, but some people might want to get ahead in school or experience school from a different perspective. If you were only going to take classes in your gap you might as well just go to college, therefore for a lot of people who choose to take classes in their gap year, they are doing it in a different country to have a study-abroad experience. There is an option to repeat your senior year of high school in a different country. This is a really cool option if you are interested in learning a different language and want a full-immersion experience to become fluent. You've already had a senior year so the classes you take might be somewhat familiar, but the challenge is now you are doing it in a language that is not your own.

Of course you need a significant amount of knowledge of that language already to be able to do this. If this option isn't for you, there are other programs designed for students to take classes at foreign institutions. Start by researching the place/school you want to attend, and find out what options that school has.

You might be planning on spending a portion of your gap year at home while you are working to save money for your adventure. You could take a class at a local university, community college or tech center if you wanted to while you are at home working. The period while you are solely working will be pretty boring and monotonous so this would be a way to get some intellectual and social stimulation during that time period. I live in Vermont and my state has a dual enrollment/continuing education program that offers discounted college courses. Obviously this varies by state but it is worth looking into if it is something you are interested in.

Working

It is likely you will have to spend some portion of your gap year working to fund the more exciting experiences you want to have. I'm not going to lie; this is not going to be a fun time period. You'll probably be working a minimum wage job that is not particularly interesting. I worked at a local market/deli where I worked as a cashier, made sandwiches and operated the ice cream window and disliked pretty much every minute of it.

The only way to get through it is to know you are doing this so you can have incredible, life-changing experiences that most people will never have. You are doing it so you can see the world and figure out what is meaningful to you, and then go to college to be prepared to make that issue/topic into a career that you will find engaging and rewarding. In essence, you are paying your dues. We all have to do it at some point.

That being said, don't discount this time period entirely. I still learned life lessons and skills during this experience. For example, I learned how to work with all different kinds of people, some more challenging than others. With those that are more difficult, I learned how to navigate those relationships/situations by giving and taking. I discovered how important it is to have at least one "work friend" that you can depend on and, let's be honest, commiserate with when needed. I figured out what makes you the employee that businesses want to hire. You'll gain all that, while earning money, and another line on your resume.

THREE

Funding Your Gap Year

Sandwiches, Teddy Bears and An Ice Cream Window

> *"Life is full of exquisite diversions."*
> - found on a gift card

Perhaps the most difficult challenge of your gap year will be funding all the amazing adventures and experiences you want to have. It is so fun to imagine and research all the possible opportunities, but one of the biggest factors to consider while planning is funding. Everyone's situation is unique when it comes to their own savings or family contribution, and there are many ways to do it.

The summer before my gap year I worked about thirty hours a week at the horse barn that I rode at, and I put away all of that money in my savings. At that point I didn't know what I was going to do with my gap year, but I knew at some point I was going to need a considerable amount of funds. When I went to D.C., I stayed in dormitory housing that was therefore fairly affordable, and my parents covered that cost for me. My dorm also provided meals, so I didn't have to buy groceries. I was fortunate that my internship offered a stipend. A stipend is monetary compensation that is less than an actual paycheck. I was lucky my internship offered this; most internships are unpaid if you don't have a degree. I also put all of that money into my savings.

I returned home from D.C. just before Christmas. I would have about six weeks before I would leave for South Africa. During that time period I got a holiday season job at the Vermont Teddy Bear Factory. The Teddy Bear Factory is exactly what it sounds like, along with a pajama company, a pajamas-that-look-like-jeans company, and a flower company. Because they have much more business during the holiday season, they hire temporary employees for this time period. This is how I ended up in their call center.

My job was to process the orders that people placed over the phone. This means that someone would call, tell me what they wished to order, and I would basically place the order for them on the website. It was the simplest job, yet I had to attend a five hour long training session beforehand. This was late November, when I was waiting in excruciating anxiety to hear back from Wake Forest University, where I had applied early decision. Every afternoon I would walk to my mailbox with my heart in my throat. I would snap open the mailbox door, scan for the large black letter (the one that acceptance letters came in, rejection letters came in a white letter), and my knees would go weak when I didn't see it.

The day I attended the training session I reluctantly had to leave before the mail had been delivered. As the Teddy Bear Factory employee droned on all I could think about was the letter, as it was late at this point. I texted my mother, hiding my phone under the table, to ask her if it had come. I discreetly checked my phone every thirty seconds, but she never responded. I couldn't shake the feeling that the letter was there.

Thirty painful minutes later, an unfamiliar woman walked into my room.

"Is there an Abby in here?" she asked in an annoyed tone.

There were two of us named Abby in the room.

"The one with the little sister with the hot dog earrings," she clarified, and said that she was outside.

I sheepishly took claim to the girl with the hot dog earrings (knowing it was my little sister) and practically sprinted out of the room, sure of what this was about. I walked out of the doors to see my mother, sister and brother jumping up and down, grinning. In my sister Haley's hand was a big black letter.

Reeling with relief at being accepted to Wake Forest, I started my job at the Teddy Factory. To be honest, it sucked. I thought about my future classmates at Wake who were working hard but basking in accomplishment as high school seniors among their friends, and here I was placing orders for people who wanted to wear pajamajeans. I knew that soon I would be in South Africa, having the most unique and special experience, but it was hard to be at such a different place in my life than others my age.

On my first day I sat in the scratchy swivel chair with my headset on, and listened to the two girls next to me discuss which store was easiest to steal from, Wal-Mart or K-Mart. I thought to myself, *I do not belong here.* Another day they needed extra help in the assembly line part of the store, so I found myself dressing teddy bears in elaborate outfits and packaging pajama orders into boxes. Again I thought to myself, *how did I get here?*

For whatever reason, customers think that because they are talking on the phone, they can be as rude as they want to the person on the other line. One wouldn't believe the amount of times I was cursed at, yelled at, treated disrespectfully, all while trying to order a Christmas teddy bear. The positive side was that I developed a sincere respect for workers serving the public, especially customer service representatives. I felt like because I was working at a call center (and not in school) people assumed I was stupid, lacked drive, or wasn't competent enough to place their online order. I constantly wanted to explain myself and why I was there, and that was frustrating. But it showed me that you never know what someone else's story is. You never know how they are struggling or what they are reaching for. But you shouldn't have to know to give that person the dignity and respect you would give any man or woman dressed in a business suit.

After being mistreated by caller after caller, when one nice person would ask me over the phone, "How are you?" before I took their order, their kindness would strike me. You hear people ask that phrase all the time and know they probably don't care about your answer, but that question can be so touching when you aren't shown that decency on the regular. It shows that you are acknowledging that employee as a person. Never underestimate the power of asking someone how their day is going or thanking them for helping you.

I used the money I had saved from my summer job at the barn, my internship, and the Teddy Bear Factory to pay for the program in South Africa, along with a contribution from my parents. My grandmother bought my plane ticket, and I will never be able to thank her enough, because without her this wouldn't have been possible. When I got there, driving from the tiny airport in middle-of-nowhere South Africa to the place we would be staying, I was surprised to see a landscape very different than I imagined it to be. When I thought of Africa I expected open, dry fields of yellow dirt. What I saw outside my window was a lush, green landscape in a thick tangle of bush. The sky was a striking blue and the hot air wrapped around me immediately after stepping off the plane. I knew every minute spent working was worth this.

When I returned from South Africa, I knew I would have to get a full-time job. I had to pay back my father for his contribution to my South Africa program, and I had the idea of the London School of Economics (LSE) rattling around in my brain. When I approached my parents about LSE, they told me that if I wanted to go I would have to fund the entire program on my own. I returned home at the end of March, and had applied to three jobs within my first week home. I was feeling major withdraw from the thrilling experience of South Africa. I missed my teammates that had grown to be like family, the excitement of our morning horseback rides, the sun that had turned my skin brown. I returned home to no friends from high school I was connected to anymore. This all lead to me feeling pretty depressed the first couple of weeks home. But I knew my gap year was not over yet, so I felt propelled to earn as much money as possible these next few months.

I ended up with a job at a market and deli. In the beginning I only worked as a cashier, starting at the "bottom level" of positions. This particular store was not very busy, so I spent most of time doing other tasks in the store like stocking grocery, cleaning, or checking expiration labels. I have never felt so unstimulated in my life. I felt nervous around my bosses, because I have a desire to please that left me frustrated and embarrassed when I made mistakes. When the weather got warmer, we opened up the ice cream window, and I got to work out there when it had customers. I liked the ice cream window much more as it was out of view of everyone else; I simply felt I did the best job when no one was watching me, waiting for me to falter. Eventually, I received a "promotion" and my responsibilities expanded to working behind the deli counter making sandwiches.

The last job I had had for a significant amount of time was at the barn I had worked and ridden at since I was thirteen years old. Therefore I knew how to do the job exceptionally well; I knew each horse inside and out. This job consisted of taking care of powerful yet fragile athletes that were worth more than some houses. I worked on my own, so I was solely responsible for making decisions and taking actions without guidance or supervision. Not only did I feed and clean them- I treated injuries, gave shots, and communicated with the vet and farrier. My boss completely trusted me, and took my opinion seriously when questions arose. The job made me feel empowered by my capability and immensely proud of my work.

This is what I was accustomed to in the workplace. Working at the market and deli was an entirely different situation. I had no prior experience in what I was doing. I felt constantly watched and scrutinized. In addition I found like at the teddy bear factory, serving the public is sometimes a thankless job. I had to constantly remind myself that I was paying my dues for the incredible experience I just had, and was making another opportunity possible.

Like I said earlier, a little bit of kindness would go a long way. One day I made a woman a sandwich, and she had asked me for my recommendation on what kind to get. I grilled a veggie sandwich, spreading apple butter and honest mustard on the whole wheat bread, and handed it over the counter to the customer. It was pouring rain that day, so the woman ate her sandwich in her car as we only had outdoor seating. About ten minutes later she came back into the store, and handed me a one dollar bill.

"Here, this a tip for making me such a great sandwich," she explained with a smile.

No one ever tipped for sandwich making, and this woman made the effort to come back inside, through the rain, to show her appreciation. That one-dollar bill and her kindness made my day.

In this experience I learned a lot about management. I saw directly how different management styles affected my desire to do a quality job. I felt how they impacted my sense of dignity and value as an employee. I learned what I want to look for in a workplace, and know how I want to be as a leader one day. I discovered what it was like to earn minimum wage and was astounded by the thought of supporting a family with my paycheck like many Americans do. It affirmed my desire work in politics and be an advocate. This is proof that every experience in your gap year- positive or negative- will expand you as a person.

Obviously, funding your gap year is going to look different for each person and their family. But if you have to earn money during some point, I will say that having at least one fellow employee that you get along with is a life-saver. Once I bonded with just one of my coworkers, my job immediately felt lighter. Not only does this make it easier to entertain yourself, it feels really good to have someone to commiserate with.

I would also strongly suggest to take advantage of any money-making opportunity you see, even if it seems small. I took every babysitting offer I got, I replied to a community advertisement looking for someone to walk their dog. I sold homemade body scrub at a craft fair. Before I went to South Africa, I entered a contest hosted by the program I was going with. I had to make a video about why I wanted to go to South Africa with the chance to win a flight voucher. I had no expectation of winning, but I did, and I would not have been able to go to London without this free flight. I volunteered to write my team's blog for for the company I went to South Africa with, and they paid me for that. I even ended up selling a few possessions I had that were worth money to fund my trip to London. No earning potential is too small, so get creative.

In conclusion, working is not going to be your favorite part of your gap year. Your (most likely) minimum wage job will be tedious; you will feel isolated at times as most people your age aren't working full time. However, working this kind of job will make you incredibly grateful for the education you are about to receive. Too many people go to college because it is what they believe they "should" do, and sit in their lectures scrolling through Facebook. (I know this for a fact, because I saw it in every one of the college classes I took when I was in high school.) Hopefully it will cause you to be more engaged and work harder in college, because you will realize just how lucky you are to be there. Your job is merely a stepping stone to the life-changing adventures you can have during your gap year and beyond that: a privileged future of higher education and careers that are stimulating and inspiring.

FOUR

"Is this seat taken?"

What I learned as an underage, ineligible to vote, intern who had a seat at the table.

On midterm election night, my friend and fellow intern and I emerged from the Metro at Union Station. The night was dark, but right in front of us was the U.S. Capitol building, lit up in its most iconic glory. I couldn't help but continuously look over at it as we walked, attempting to walk slower so I could savor the moment. We passed a group of slightly intoxicated people, linked in arms, singing some chant about the grand 'ole party. My friend and I groaned, still feeling the disappointment shared in the room of the election party we had just returned from at a strictly progressive firm. I was feeling so much in that moment: awe of how I had fallen in love with this city, pride in the work I had done related to this election, concern for the ideals I valued and the jeopardy they were now in with the outcome of this election. I was feeling sad that my time here would end in just a few weeks. I felt grown-up.

This was a complete transformation from how I felt when I arrived in D.C. To be blunt, in the beginning I hated everything. I complained about the constant noise and bustle of the city, about the crowdedness of the train cars. I didn't want to eat dinner with the other girls in my dorm. When I arrived at Lake Research Partner's office on my first day, I was petrified. My dad walked me there my first day, and so together we arrived at the glass doors of the office building. He pulled open the door to open it for me, and off went a blaring alarm. The noise sent me into a panic. A man came running to the door, pressed a button, and then walked away without saying a word to us. This was my first taste of the fast-paced, high pressure environment that is LRP. While this interaction only increased my fear, I grew to really respect and appreciate this environment. We were doing serious and important work and there were high expectations of everyone, and I was humbled to be a part of it.

My first week I, like all other new interns, had to work at the front desk the whole week (later on we would switch off by day). This meant that in addition to all your other intern tasks, you had to work as a receptionist. I had the hardest time figuring out how to answer the phone, then transfer the line to someone else in the office. You had to 1) ask for the name of the person who was calling, 2) look up the extension of the person they were asking for, 3) call that person and tell them who was on the line, and 4) finally transfer the call. Doesn't sound too difficult right? I would forget the name of the person that had called, not be able to understand them, call the wrong extension, accidentally hang up on the person calling, etc. Within the first twenty minutes of my very first day, I had run into the office of the other interns twice to embarrassingly ask them yet another question about the stupid phone. A few weeks later I had a systematic way of answering the phone mastered and all the extensions memorized, and it was hard to believe that task had nearly put me in tears the first day.

My next obstacle that first day was lunch. I had assumed that all the interns would eat lunch together, in the break room or something like that. Around 12:30 I took the peanut butter sandwich I packed to the break room. A few minutes after sitting down, an analyst walked in and (nicely) said they were having a meeting in there, and so I had to leave. Not knowing what to do, I awkwardly stood in the office kitchen to finish my lunch. By the second day I realized no one at LRP really takes a lunch break, there is no time for that. Instead, they eat lunch at their desks while they continue to work, a practice I soon adopted with my work load.

Later that first week, I somehow made the mistake of accidentally printed about two hundred copies of something I only needed to print once. The copy room was daunting to me; it was filled with expensive machines that were not simple to use at first. I was standing in the copy room, waiting for the document I had tried to print, thinking *wow, why is some printing three million copies of something?* I lifted one page up to see what it was, and was horrified to find it was my document! *How the heck did that happen?* I thought.

I rushed to press the "cancel" bottom and quickly gathered up the papers. It was the very end of the day, but I had to stay until 9pm that night for an intern training. I was exhausted, hungry and frustrated but knew I had to do something quick as there was one woman in the office who was very concerned about the environment and therefore appointed herself as the monitor of printed paper. She was a little intimidating anyways, and I knew if I just dumped all these papers in the nearest recycling bin I'd be hearing about it from her.

Just then, one of the other interns walked in. She would become one of my few friends in D.C., but at this point we barely knew each other. Holding a massive pile of papers in my hands, I had no choice but to confess my mistake to her.
"No worries, we'll fix this," she said, not even phased. Those first few weeks I was so worried about making mistakes and proving I was capable; hearing those words I took a huge breath.

Her plan was to divide the stack into little piles, and deposit each smaller pile in a different recycling bin around the office. That way, no one would notice anything strange. We split up and nonchalantly walked around the office, slipping the paper into bins. I quickly realized having an ally like that in the workplace is invaluable.

As an intern one of my main tasks was proofing reports and presentations. There was text proofing, when you would check the document for grammar and spelling errors before it was sent to a client. There was also number proofing. These reports would include many graphs and tables, and it was our job as intern to make sure the numbers listed on those diagrams were correct. This meant we had to use a "banner book:" a giant binder of, on average, seven hundred pages of numbers. You had to figure out where the number you were checking was in the book, find its location, and then check to make sure the number was correct in the report. Depending on the length of the report, this could take hours or days and was an incredibly meticulous process.

Another project we would be assigned was known as "clips." An analyst would need information on a certain topic, for example the opinion of Hispanic voters in a particular election. Our job was to research and find quality articles on this topic, put them together and send them to the analyst. Sometimes the topic would be easy to find. Other times it would require some serious digging. I felt a lot of pressure to deliver quality articles, so this really tested my persistence in finding information during the times when they didn't come up easily.

My favorite task was going to presentations and taking notes, then writing summaries on the event. I would attend presentations, debates, and other meetings, take notes on what was said, and then write a summary on the event that would be given to the president of the firm. I got to go to really cool presentations and listen to very impressive people speak. For example I attended the "Wednesday Group" meeting at AFL-CIO, a weekly meeting where some of D.C.'s most powerful pollsters, analysts and other professionals in politics get together. When I entered the room at AFL-CIO's headquarters, there was a massive wooden table, and other doctor's office-style seats off to the side. Tentative, I chose one of the doctor office seats off to the side. When the meeting began to fill, I saw the main seats weren't full, so I nervously took a seat at the table. Before the meeting began, I had to introduce myself. Several people smiled at me, as, at 17, I was probably the youngest person to ever sit at their Wednesday Group table.

One morning I was sitting at my computer when a notification popped up in my email; I was supposed to attend a presentation at the Center for American Progress— in ten minutes. Suddenly, I remembered offering to take notes on this presentation about the challenges working mothers face. I didn't know where this building was, so I knew I couldn't walk. Flying out of the office, I frantically searched for a cab. Once in a car I googled the address of the location, and ended up being dropped off at the wrong address. I raced out of the building, and followed the map app on my phone to get to CAP, discovering thankfully it was right around of the corner. I got to the room just in time, sat down, and discovered I didn't bring a notebook or a pen. I felt a flash a panic and then moved into solution mode. I dug through my purse and didn't find a pen, but did find an old brochure I had collected at some point. I accepted this was all I had to take notes on. I embarrassingly asked the receptionist to borrow a pen, and proceeded to take my notes in between the text of my brochure. In the end I was still able to write a good summary, and you would never have known the notes were taken in tiny letters on that brochure.

I worked long hours; my hours were technically 9-6 but I usually left closer to 7, some nights staying as late as 9pm. The atmosphere was intense and the pace was incredibly fast, but it was all worth it as I was working for candidates and organizations that mattered to me.

Weekend in D.C. were tough for me. For the last ten years of my life, my weekends were filled with horses. Especially in the last five years, I spent every Saturday and Sunday from 7am-5pm in a barn. What did other people do on weekends? I really didn't know. I decided to take up running. Now that I sat at a desk from 9-6:30, I took to running not because I wanted to but because I was desperate for exercise. My dorm was located on Capitol Hill, right down the street from the Supreme Court. So every weekend I would go from the Capitol Building, down the Mall to the Lincoln Memorial and back. The first time I did it I would stop to look at each memorial. I didn't feel like the tourists that gathered around the monuments in their matching t-shirts, but I didn't quite feel like the other runners, clearly D.C. residents, either. By the end of the ten weeks I could run the entire 6 mile route, but the magnificence of the Mall never got old for me. It was a routine I grew to love. At the end of one of these runs I realized one of the lessons I learned in D.C.: there are parts of yourself that you have yet to discover. We think we know ourselves pretty well, and so we spend most our energy trying to figure other people out. Spoiler alert; we are wrong. I don't believe people change- but I do believe that we discover new parts of ourselves. This happens on different depths. For example, I found putting on my sneakers became one of the best parts of my day. On a deeper level, I discovered hidden strength, but also buried vulnerabilities. When I came home I was not be a different person, but rather a more *complete* version of myself.

But like I said, weekends were hard, mainly because I didn't have a peer group I belonged in. I wasn't in high school anymore, but I wasn't in college either. I was years younger than the other interns in my office. While I made two great friends (one that went to Georgetown University, and one that was also an intern at my office) that I spent some time with, I spent much of my time alone. I filled my days by going grocery shopping at the store that took longer to walk to, or doing things that had familiarity like going to Panera Bread, which became my Sunday evening ritual. I started a new television series, I researched parks that I visited with a good book, but it made me realize, sometimes in life, you have to walk alone. I wasn't in DC with a "gap year" program. I didn't have any family or friends in the area. I had to navigate a city I was not at all familiar with. I was years younger than the other girls living in my dorm. And I was at a completely different place in my life than the other interns in my office. All of these factors lead to me feeling pretty isolated, especially at first. At times I wished that I could be in the same position that my friends back home were in: their senior year of high school, still living in their childhood homes, at the same school with familiar faces. Instead, I was trying to follow along in staff meetings. But in the end, I had a fantastic experience, and I wouldn't have had that experience if I hadn't chosen to do something different, even if I had to do it alone. It was the first time I realized that the beaten path is overrated!

The social experiences I had were eye-opening and to be frank, humbling. They gave me another big realization I had during my time there, that there is always going to be someone smarter than you. Prior to coming to DC, I was a big fish in a small pond. In school, I was the one who raised my hand because I always knew the answer, the one who aced the test without having to study. Within the first week of my internship I found myself in conversations that I could not contribute to-because I didn't know what they were talking about. (This would happen many more times.) These were often conversations that would happen at work between me and the other interns. We could debate current political events or discuss our opinions on foreign affairs and for the first time in my life, I was hesitant to say anything. I am glad I had this humbling experience before college, where this will certainly happen to me again. And I hope it does; now when these situations come up, I am taking mental notes.

I learned to pay close attention to the people that are older than you. Yes, I learned a lot from my internship. But what I learned about from my office was- political polling. Important stuff, but not the most important. I learned as much as, or maybe even more from, the people around me- especially the other interns. The other interns were young enough that we became friends on a more personal level than just work colleagues, and from them I learned so many life lessons I started to write them all down. People love to give advice- and they were eager to fill me in on what they considered to be the most critical "life's truths." The topics ranged from boys, friends, college, eating habits, safety tips, office etiquette, when and when not to say you are sorry. I soaked up their knowledge like a sponge and they fed it to me like candy.

I have a friend who is a sophomore at Georgetown University (who also has taken a gap year). I experienced this realization again when she invited me to attend their debate society meeting. This was a group at Georgetown that meets once a week to debate controversial issues. I remember walking into the room of the first meeting I attend; my eyes rotated around the room, trying to take in my surroundings. I looked up, and saw there were about four floors of bookcases spiraling upward. But these were not bookcases like I had ever seen at a library; each shelf contained rows of leather-bound thick books, their covers in shades of red, orange, gold and navy. Around the room were several figurehead statues, and a coat of arms hung on the wall. Directly in front of me was a tall, cathedral-style window. It was dark by the time we had gotten there, but I know it was overlooking a green. Outside I could see several lights glowing from the oil- lit lamps. I was in the Riggs Library at Georgetown University.

After introducing me to a few people, Ashley and I sat down in the front row. She noticed me still gawking at the enchanting room.

"Do you want to go upstairs and look around? We have a few minutes until it starts."

I did, but I did not want to make it obvious to the people around me that I was an outsider, so I said no. This was just another Thursday night to them.

The president of the group entered the room, he was announced and everyone stood up and greeted him with a "haza!"

Tonight they were debating whether the famed baseball player Barry Bonds, who had broken numerous records, should have been inducted into the Hall of Fame even after he was found to have been using steroids. After the two keynote speakers made arguments for both sides, the floor was opened for the society members to speak. As more brilliant people stood to offer their opinions, I thought to myself that this was what I've been longing for my whole life, to be surrounded by people like this.

This is another one of the greatest gifts D.C. gave me: it made me really excited for college. I went through the college search and application process a year early, and I wasn't at all ready. I had to be encouraged to go on college tours, I disliked them so much. Everything about college scared me, and I didn't feel excited about it in the way I knew I should. This all changed for me during my time in D.C. Not only did my internship and living on my own make me feel confident about leaving home, but moments like the ones I had at this debate society opened my eyes to all the amazing things I have to look forward to.

One night I was in a cab, driving home from Georgetown. I was making small-talk with the cab driver, and he asked me what I wanted to study when I go to college next year. Caught up in the whimsical dream of college I have, especially after spending time with Georgetown students, I enthusiastically answered that I wanted to study lots of things-the intersection of neurology and political science, but also French, philosophy, literature, even theology! Without reservation he told me no- I shouldn't do that. He explained to me about how he had moved to America to attend college, but still couldn't find a decent job, even though he graduated with a degree. Therefore he urged me to choose a more practical major- economics or pre-med.

Everyone knows something you don't know, or sees a perspective you can't see. This means you must listen, listen, listen. Everyone's story is important. This includes your work colleagues', your best friend's, your new friends', the president of your firm's, and the cab driver's who took you home. Listening may not change your path, but it will always give you something to think about. The second part of this lesson is that in order to listen to someone else's story, you must forget about your own for a little while. Our thoughts are constantly dominated by how we are going to get ahead, what matters to us, what concerns us. Sometimes I was so consumed with my own worries that "my story" was the only one I could think about. Pay most attention the ones like are most unlike your own, and the ones most like what you want yours to become. It's free wisdom.

I really liked my morning commute to work. I dressed in my "work clothes," and followed the crowd of businessmen/women, policy makers, lawyers, CEOs, and other 9-5 workers through Union Station with my alternative Pandora station streaming through my headphones. I was only an intern, but I could travel my morning commute and share a feeling of purpose with my fellow Metro passengers. On that election night, when the Republicans swept the Senate and the House, I was hit by a feeling that said *I was there*. It mattered, because there I was, at my firm's election party, feeling the disappointment that every progressive felt that night- even though I was the only one that couldn't indulge in the highly-acclaimed margarita machine. As I got off at Union Station on my way home that night, and passed the Capitol lit up at night, again- *I was there*. My experience in D.C. taught me to take every opportunity to be a part of something that is bigger than yourself. I learned that while personal success feels great, a shared cause feels *monumental*. And I couldn't even vote yet.

FIVE

Bush Rules

South Africa: Bush House, Horses and Lions

Interaction with a wild animal is hard to describe, as I cannot describe it from the point of view readers would understand, from the point of a view of a human observing wild. Because a moment like that breaks down the barrier between wild and tame; for a moment we felt just as wild, just as vulnerable, and just as sacred as the animal in front of us.

--AT, January 30, 2015

Above is a journal entry I wrote while I was in South Africa. I wrote it about the night we saw the elephants in our yard that I described earlier. I went to South Africa to volunteer on a game reserve and in the local community. A game reserve is an area of land that is protected so wildlife can live naturally. Many game reserves have lodges for guests to stay and go on safaris. The game reserve I was at was called Kwa Madwala; it had an upscale lodge for safari guests and a much more rustic house that volunteers stayed in, known as

Bush House. Bush House was my home for ten weeks, along with fifteen other eighteen and nineteen year-olds. There was one other American, twelve from England, one from Switzerland and one from Holland. There was an element of horseback riding to the program; we rode every morning around the reserve, exposed to the lions, elephants, everything. Our main volunteering task was to remove snares from the bush. The "bush" is the terrain of South Africa- it is a thick tangle of thorny trees and bushes. We would search through it and remove snares that poachers used to catch animals. Snares are loops of wire; poachers attach one end to a tree, and the other end in a loop to catch an animal's neck or leg. When the animal pulls back against the snare, it grows tighter and most of the time kills them.

We would do our "anti-poaching" (our term for the snare removal task) early in the morning, beginning at 4:30am, to catch the snares the poachers had put out during the night (hopefully) before they caught any animals. We would take the horses, ride to the location, and then get off and lead our horses while we were navigating through the bush that is too thick to ride through. One of the first mornings we did this, we were warned that the lions were somewhere near the area we would be searching, and so we had to be aware. Theoretically there should have been an adult, our group leader, riding leader, or a member of the anti-poaching team with us at all times. But we were a big group, and we wouldn't find much with everyone walking in one line, so naturally our group would disperse. I was riding with two other girls when I spotted a snare. I jumped off my horse to take the snare off the tree, while the two other girls waited behind me on their horses. Right in front of us was a giant bush, and all of a sudden the bush began to loudly rustle. Then we heard grunting noises- clearly the sound of an animal struggling. I thought immediately of the warning we had gotten that morning about the lions, and thought for sure this was a lion making a kill. My friend behind me saw a flash of brown and yelled, "BABY LION!" My chest surged. I have never jumped on a horse so fast, and actually mounted without putting my foot in the stirrup first- a feat that would probably be physically impossible had it not been for the adrenaline rush I got out of fear.

The noises in the bush were not a lion, or else I probably would not be here to write this book. The noise we heard was an impala (a small antelope) being caught in a snare. Luckily we were there and were able to cut the impala out of the snare and save its life. During anti-poaching we would occasionally come across impalas we had not been able to save. An impala's twisted neck in a snare, eyes still open, flies covering its corpse, is a heartbreaking image I will never forget.

We also did tasks known as "conservation." These were mainly maintenance projects around the reserve. We would cut down overgrown trees and bushes, or fix things around the reserve. Our main task was to dig a trench along the road, to collect the rain that falls during South Africa's rainy season. Digging the trench in the heat of a South African afternoon was intense. I remember one afternoon we joked that we were living in the novel Holes. Another afternoon we had to end early because one of us had accidentally chopped down a tree that contained a wasp nest- and we were so grateful!

Riding horses was one of the main elements of the program (and the reason why I chose it.) Before leaving I had daydreams of us galloping across the plains of Africa, tracking a herd of buffalo or a wounded rhino. I was intrigued by the idea of riding in the bush, but I had no idea what to expect. When we got to the stables our first day, I looked down at my nice boots, already covered in red dirt. We met Louis, our riding guide. He looked rough and intimidating in every way, from his pointed chin and harsh eyes, to the cigarette always in his right hand. But I wasn't afraid of him, instead I thought to myself that if there was anyone leading me through the African bush, I wanted it to be this man.

As we got to know Louis, we found he fulfilled that first impression we had of him. He would show up to the stables each day on his motorcycle- on which he could spin, jump over objects, and perform wheelies of course. He told us stories of coming face-to face with lions in the bush while on foot. He chased poachers. He knew how to milk snakes for their venom. He feared nothing that was out there- not the lions that could kill you with the swipe of a paw, the elephants that will stampede a group of horses, or the snakes that will end your life in twelve minutes after a bite. But we also saw how he would speak to his horse Spirit when he thought no one was watching. One day, we were riding along the fence line that bordered a sugar cane farm. He called over to the workers in Afrikaans, and they brought us several canes of sugar. He taught us how to bite off a piece and suck the sugar out of it, then spit out the remaining plant. He told us about how he and his brother would chew sugar cane and ride their horse bareback when they were kids. Even in the beginning, we knew Louis would have done anything to keep us safe.

Next we met the horses, whom I would soon discover were nothing like any horse I had met before. They were tougher, covered in ticks that I would remove before riding even though I knew they'd be back the next day. They would scramble over rocks, jump down ditches and canter through thorns, never stopping. Meanwhile the horses I had at home were only allowed a small square of grass (no holes, no mud, flat), that they were turned loose in only after being outfitted in boots on each leg and a sheet that repelled bugs. The horses in South Africa amazed me; they had unmatchable stamina in the intense heat and could reach a speed I had never experienced before. We would race them on the way home, and there was this moment when you would let the reins loose and stand up in your seat. You could signal them to go into this whole other gear, and we would be galloping so fast I could no longer feel their legs moving under me.

Before we rode that first day, we spoke with Louis, the other two riding guides that accompanied us and took care of the horses, and the manager of the reserve. He explained to us that they didn't bring guns while we were out riding, because they had "awareness" instead. My face was expressionless but inside I felt a flutter of nerves. The image of a snarling lion charging us popped in my head; what was awareness going to do for us then? It became a line we would joke about amongst ourselves later: "Don't worry, we have awareness!"

It turned out that my nervousness was pretty legitimate. To put it mildly, safety standards in South Africa were a bit lower than what I was used to. The safety vest we were told to bring never made it out of my suitcase. I had to accept the fact that I had very little control while riding; when the lead horse took off, there was no way to stop or slow down your horse if you wanted to. I was used to competitive riding, where every movement is deliberate and every step is controlled.

One day I was riding a pony that was inappropriately named "Johnny-Be-Good." We would ride on dirt paths that were bordered on either side by the bush. We would be single file or side-by-side and the horses were pretty intent on staying in a group (safety in numbers!) Except for Johnny- who had a scary habit of randomly breaking away from the group and charging into the bush. We didn't know why he did it, we couldn't predict when he would do it. So as we were galloping along, Johnny suddenly turned to the left and together we plunged into the bush. I frantically attempted to turn him but it had been raining that day and my reins were wet, so I couldn't get a good grip on them. When I couldn't get him to turn I leaned over the side, trying to grab his bit to at least stop him. All the while he was still running aimlessly around the bush as thorns and branches tore up my arms. I was yelling for help and for Louis. Going through my mind was *this is it, this is how I could die.* I knew that if we came across a lion, leopard, the elephants, a rhino, a snake- any animal- on our own it would surely attack us. I couldn't tell where we were, but suddenly I saw the path- Johnny had run back! I looked down the path and saw my group, and felt a surge of relief. They yelled to me, but I couldn't even hear what they said, as Johnny galloped right across the path and back into the bush on the other side.

Here we go again I thought as my heart beat furiously. As we ventured further from the group, I knew I had to make a decision. I could hold on, because I had a better chance of getting away if I met another animal while I was on horseback, but the distance was growing and I didn't know when he would stop. Or I could jump off and abandon this crazy ride, but that would mean I would be on foot in the bush-alone. Not wanting to waste another second, I kicked both feet out of the stirrups and jumped. I hit the ground, jumped to my feet and started to run the direction I thought the path was in, never looking back at Johnny, who never even slowed down.

I made it to the path, and my teammates shouted to Louis, who was in the bush looking for me. Now I didn't know how I was going to get back without a horse. Without hesitating, Timba, one of the other guides, dismounted his horse and handed him to me.

"But how will Timba get back?" I asked.

"He'll walk," Louis answered.

I didn't understand, the thought of being alone in the bush on foot, exposed to lions and leopards, made me terrified for him.

"He'll be fine," Louis said, without an ounce of concern.

"And what about Johnny-Be-Good, are we going to look for him?" He was a prey animal, a lion would want to eat him!

"Nah, he'll come back to the stables eventually, Johnny-Be-Bastard."

There were some dicey moments, but in the end there is no feeling more exhilarating than galloping a horse; there were moments riding in South Africa in which I felt happier than I have ever felt. There were times I wanted to whoop out loud at how *alive* I felt. There is nothing to compare it to.

The other element of our volunteer work was volunteering in the orphanage in the community. The community is a township- housing areas that were set up during the Apartheid. This means the community is very poor and affected by AIDS/HIV, drug use, and other like issues. Almost sixty percent of the orphans at the orphanage lost their parents to AIDS/HIV. Every time we went there we had to make sure any open wound was covered by several band-aids to ensure we didn't contract AIDS, as some of the kids we would play with were suffering from it also. The first time we were instructed to do this we looked around at each other nervously and our group leader bellowed, "Welcome to Africa!"

There was a newly-built schoolhouse at the orphanage, so our main task was to paint it's walls. But many of our days at the orphanage were spent simply playing with the kids. These kids don't receive much attention, so it was really exciting for them to have us come. As soon as our car would drive in to the community, kids would pour out of houses and chase after our car. As soon as we got out, there would be a child attached to your leg, your arm, begging to be picked up. I realized they mainly just wanted touch- they wanted to be carried, to sit in your lap, to play with your hair. It was overwhelming at first, and we left sticky with sweat, some of which was our own, some of which was the kids' that had been physically attached to us for the last hours.

I'll admit I had a favorite child. I don't know her name as she rarely spoke, but I could tell she was about four or five years old. Most of the kids would go crazy for the balls, bubbles, and crayons we brought, but she never wanted to play with any of it. I would try to engage her with chalk or a wind-up toy, but all she wanted was to sit on my lap-silently. I felt I lucked out with this; while everyone else was running around in the heat or getting their hair pulled out all I had to do was sit with a sweet little girl in my lap.

Everyone would always comment on her as she was striking in two ways; one being how beautiful of a child she is. She has the widest eyes, perfectly symmetrical features and sweet, full lips. Secondly, they commented on the tragic look on her face that never left. I wondered about what horrible event she had witnessed that rendered her speechless and with this sorrowful look. It made me feel a desperate desire to smother her in nurture. I made sure to find her as soon as we got to the orphanage each time. First I would take off the many layers of clothing she would be wearing- I would find her in fleece sweaters when it was ninety-five degrees, on top of another shirt. I would tie the fleece around her waist, worried that other kids would take it if I didn't keep it attached to her, as at this place it was clearly survival of the fittest. As soon as she saw me she would lift her arms above her head, asking to be picked up. I would carry her somewhere to sit. Other kids would attempt to climb in my lap and she would respond to them with a swift slap. I knew I should tell her not to hit other kids, but I wanted her to know me as the one person who only cared about her.

The only day I ever heard her speak was when I was carrying her past a sign on the classroom wall that had the letters of the alphabet. She reached out and pointed at the letters and began to recite, "A, B, C, D, E, F, G" in perfect English. I was so shocked I almost dropped her on the ground.

Firstly, this was the first and only time she had uttered any sound. Secondly, none of the kids there spoke English, they would jabber away at us in their native language. One of the caretakers there must have taught them the letters in English, but I'll never know more as those were the first and last words (not even words, letters) she ever said to me. Sometimes I think of her and wish I could fly back and whisk her away from the yard of dust I met her in.

The tragic truth is that the two most common things people associate with the continent of Africa are the wildlife and poverty. Yes, I witnessed extreme poverty in South Africa and Mozambique. It struck me most profoundly one night in Mozambique. We were driving in an open vehicle back to the house we were staying at there. It was dusk and there was one of the most magnificent sunsets I've ever seen. We were driving on a road that had a line of trees in between us and the coast. Every time there was a break in the trees, we could catch a glimpse of the sun falling over the ocean. It took my breath away. It made me believe the world was magnificent.

On the other side of the road was a scattering of houses. I use the term "houses," but these are not structures like you are picturing. They were barely shacks, some made of collapsing wood, some of a cardboard-like product with newspaper stuffed into the holes. Around these buildings there were women and young children; I didn't see any men and I don't know where they were. As I looked into their faces, I was hit by this thought: *they can't leave*. The only difference between them and I was luck. I was merely lucky I was born into my family in America, and not on the dirt floor of this shack in Mozambique. I didn't do anything to deserve this starkly different start in life. *What if one of these women wanted to go to college?,* I thought to myself. How would they get there, they don't go to any form of school at all. There isn't even a school around here that they could go to if they wanted to. They are destined to grow up too quickly, get married, have babies.

I felt immediate guilt for these thoughts, like I shouldn't be assuming my life was better than theirs. But I couldn't get over the fact that *they can't leave.* These cardboard shacks were not cardboard shacks to them, they were reality, an inescapable reality.

Upon leaving South Africa, I no longer think of Africa as a *poor* continent. Africa is rich with the beauty of those sunsets in Mozambique, the grandness of its unique wildlife, the spirit of its people. But I did leave with the sobering realization that not all people on this Earth are born with an equal chance. And because much has been given to me, much is expected of me.

The most amazing animal interactions I had in South Africa were with lions. The first lion we ever saw was a young male in Kruger National Park. After two weeks in South Africa we still hadn't seen one, so this was a much-anticipated event. Our game vehicles were driving down a path, and there he was, lying on the side of the road. We were able to drive right next to him, without him caring one bit. He was just beginning to grow a mane with only a few scrappy hairs on the top of his head. Despite his young age he already had small scars scattering his face from fights with other lions. His mouth was open as he was panting, giving us a view of his teeth that I could imagine crushing a poor impala. We sat there, no more than three feet from this lion, and our group leader reminded us to keep our limbs inside of the car.

What struck me were his eyes. Lions have eyes like amber; eyes that take your breath away. I could feel my heart beating out of my chest as I continued to stare.

One of the last lions I saw in South Africa was chasing after me. We were galloping the horses down a dry riverbed, a path of sand that is flanked either side by thick bush. Suddenly we saw one of the lionesses run across the riverbed about thirty feet in front of us. We pulled up our horses immediately. I was shocked, the only other time we had seen the lions while riding we had been tracking them and therefore the sighting was expected and, to a degree, controlled. Louis, the ranger that guided our rides, rode ahead to see where she had gone. At this point we knew she was the larger of the two lionesses at Kwa Madwala, the one with four cubs, making her fairly aggressive. Feeling nervous but more excited I looked around at my teammates, and I could see in their faces they were feeling the same thing. Louis returned and reported that he didn't see her and therefore she must have run off. We rode on at a slow canter with Louis in the lead. The horses could smell the lion and where she had been; their nostrils were flaring and they would turn their heads in the direction of the scent. I could feel the apprehension in Maximus, the horse I was riding.

Often the horses would detect the presence of a lion before we could. I remember one day we were galloping along a trail, and suddenly Louis' lead horse Spirit abruptly stopped, causing the rest of the group to follow suit. We looked down and at our feet were the clear outlines of lions' paws. That being said, the only reason I felt safe riding in the bush was because of Louis. This man had faced lions on horseback and on foot too many times to count. He didn't carry a gun while we were riding, he said if a lion charged one of us he would simply charge the lion head on, whether he was on the back of a horse or not. Every day for ten weeks Louis brought us back to the stables safely, and we knew he would do anything to keep it that way. In turn, we trusted our lives with him every day.

Therefore I didn't hesitate in following him along the riverbed. I don't know if words can do justice in describing the next moment, but I will try. Out of nowhere, the lioness appeared on the riverbank on our right, less than ten feet away from us. She was standing tall in her power and malice and she roared- she roared and it made a noise that reached inside of us. It was a full-blown, animal-documentary-worthy roar, a noise we hadn't ever heard, let alone from a few feet away. Louis yelled, "RUN, GET OUT OF HERE," which was alarming, because the past ten weeks we had been told that the worst thing you can do if you meet a lion is run. But I knew

Louis had more experience with lions than anyone, so if he was telling us to run, I better book it. The horse in front of me darted to the left, and with that I gave Maximus a hard kick to go forward, knowing that the worst thing that could happen would be the horses to scatter. One girl told us afterwards that the lioness had chased after us for a bit, but I never looked back.

Louis explained that she wasn't going to attack us in a group, she only roared to give us a serious warning as her cubs were probably nearby. Looking back, I don't remember feeling afraid in that moment, because I had such a rush of adrenaline. Once we had gotten a good distance away and slowed to a walk, it took us all a while to get our breath back. When we did we could barely contain our excitement; we grilled Louis on what would have happened if one of us had fallen off (to which he responded, "I would have charged the lion") what would have happened if he had fallen off (still would have charged the lion), but mostly just talked about how that was one of the most amazing experiences of our lives so far. Thank you South Africa, I don't know how anything I experience in the future can compare to that.

Every animal interaction we had showed me that wild nature is sacred, and we are connected to it. There were so many breathtaking moments with the wild animals in South Africa. On horseback, we would share dusk with a rhino mother and her calf grazing a few feet away. We would gallop straight through a herd of zebra. I would look into a lion's amber eyes and let them take my breath away. In these moments, I never felt like I was just "observing" these animals as one would do in a zoo. I was in awe of their presence, and even more in awe of the reality that I was sharing it. My feet touched the same dirt path, we breathed the same air around us, we felt the same sun warm our skin.

Over and over again we were told "only prey runs." This phrase would be used when a ranger was reminding us what to do if you encounter a lion or other predator on foot. If you run away, you are mimicking the predator's prey, and so their instinct is to chase after and attack you. Even though this was drilled into our heads, when situations came up, instinct took over.

We spent two nights camping in Kruger National Park. Our campsite was fenced in, and at night we could watch the hyenas come right up to the other side of the fence. We would sit, speaking only in whispers, and watch them sniff around the fence, attracted by the smell of our dinner. Hyenas have massive shoulders and small heads, giving them a monster-like appearance. I felt a combination of fear and mesmerization being this close to such a creature. As we stared, transfixed by their presence, the rangers told us stories about vicious hyena attacks on humans ("You know the guy at the gas station with only one ear? Hyena.")

Our campsite was meant to be fenced in so that animals were kept out. We slept in tents, and there was a separate bathroom facility. One night I, along with two other girls, was brushing my teeth when we heard the unmistakable laughing-call of a hyena. I felt a shiver along my spine. It's eeriness rang so loud we joked that the hyena was right outside of the bathroom. We finished in the bathroom and I along with another girl started to walk back to our tents. As soon as we walked outside, she stopped abruptly and pointed, grabbing my arm. I looked up and saw the unmistakable silhouette of a hyena right in front of us, inside the camp, less than fifteen feet away! We didn't say a word to each other, I think I screamed, and together we sprinted back inside the bathroom and locked ourselves in a bathroom stall.

Even though we didn't apply the "only prey runs" philosophy in that moment, this phrase struck me as I think it's a policy you can apply to life in general. When you are confronted with a problem, it needs to be faced head-on. Running from it is neither wise nor effective, because the problem will eat you.

I would often stop and marvel at the fact that I was living in this wild, incredible place. One day at Bush House, I walked to the clothing line with my bag of wet clothes and sweat forming above my upper lip and at my hair line. The clothing line was at the edge of the "bush"- the area where we were forbidden to walk in unsupervised or even walk near at night. You couldn't see much but thick trees and bushes but you could hear the orchestra of insects humming and you could feel the tension that comes with knowing what inhabits it. I was looking down at my feet, navigating the grass that was nothing like the grass at home. This grass was rough and tangled and unpredictable.

I started to hang my clothes up on the line and almost laughed out loud at myself in these surroundings. I was thinking of how last time I used this laundry bag, I was carrying it to the laundry room of the dormitory I was living in Washington, D.C. The room was air conditioned and held rows of white washing and drying machines that stood tall in their modernity. My days were filled with speeding trains that carried me to a skyscraper building in which I spent my day looking at a computer screen and checking numbers. Everything was predicted, scheduled, measured, calculated and checked again to make sure the predicting, scheduling, measuring and calculating was done correctly.

Where I was now, the grass grew as tall as it wanted. The temperature rose as high as it wanted. The wildebeest roamed where they wanted; last night where they wanted was underneath this clothes line. Who was I, hanging up my laundry in the African bush, with my burnt face sweating in this kind of sun I hadn't met before?

While the hyena moment was terrifying, it was the essence of one of my favorite things about South Africa: the unpredictability. One night we were driving home from visiting an animal rehabilitation center, and witnessed the wildest thunderstorm I've ever seen. The sky was a purple color that would be lit by elaborate forks of lightning that reached all the way to the ground. When we got home we discovered the power was out. This meant more than no lights or fan for sleeping; at Bush House when the power went out, there was no running water. We ate dinner by flashlight, piled up our dirty dishes that we couldn't wash, and went to bed without showering off the sweat from the 109 degree day.

I woke up the next morning, went to the bathroom, and the toilet didn't flush. I was surprised the power was still out, our usual power outages lasted no more than eight hours. That morning at breakfast one of the rangers explained that in the storm the elephants had pushed over the power lines, and because it was Friday morning, the power lines wouldn't be fixed until Monday afternoon. At first, we didn't even believe him. At home it would be inconceivable to leave people without power or running water for four days. Then, we began to panic a little. We already had no clean dishes, our toilets didn't flush, our phones were out of battery so we had no flashlights, and our collective smell was probably lethal.

Our morning task was to make cement and use it to fix several things around the house. Mainly, we were putting in poles for the fencing we were putting around the vegetable patch we were growing for the community. As we worked, we planned how we were going to survive the next few days. We planned a trip to town to get paper plates and plastic utensils, created a system of using pool water to flush toilets, and figured out how we were going to cook meals. We ended up having fun doing it; the challenge made our day more exciting and we saw it as part of the adventure. The power ended up coming back early, but those twenty-four hours without it showed how adversity brings people together.

Our group went to Mozambique for three nights, so we had to cross the border and change currency. Before we got to the border, our van stopped at a gas station/strip mall so we could withdraw cash and change currency. It was the sketchiest place I've ever seen, and our group leader didn't tell us where the ATM or currency exchange was located, let alone come with us. We ended up wandering around as a group, eventually finding an ATM and then changing our money with a woman in the parking lot. We had no idea what rate she was giving us, because of course she spoke a different language. This is just to show how living abroad is one problem solving exercise after another. Challenges made our group closer; it allowed for natural leaders to step forward, collaborative thinking and cooperation in executing solutions to occur, and appreciation for one another to develop.

South Africa changed me, but not in a way that is tangible or concrete. It didn't make me want to have a career in wildlife conservation, or move to Africa, or something like that. It's imprint in me was more subtle, more internal. Since I have returned home people have told me that I seem happier, that I seem more relaxed. That is traceable, as South Africa certainly taught me how to slow down. At home, every minute of my day is scheduled, and before 9pm, I've probably spent every minute doing something I deemed to be "productive." In South Africa, there were many hours of the day to simply lay in the sun, read a book, sit in the pool, chat, watch a movie, etc. Often we didn't know what we would be doing later that day, or the next day. Nothing *ever* happened on time. It is part of South African culture to not be concerned about these things. In the beginning I was uncomfortable with this amount of "free" time and relaxed planning. But with nothing to do but adjust, I eventually really enjoyed these hours I took to just do something I wanted. As ridiculous as it sounds, I learned there are no serious repercussions to not being on time, and if you don't accomplish anything for a couple hours, that's ok too. There is value in taking time to self-reflect, lose yourself in a book, have a conversation. It is during those hours that I wrote several of the passages in this book- not with the goal of publishing a book, but just writing because I wanted to.

One morning we were riding the horses when Louis told us to dismount; he wanted to show us something and we had to get off the path and go through the bush to find it. We got off the horses and followed him through the thorns and branches. I really didn't want to get off; I was already sticky with sweat and wasn't in the mood to pull thorns out of my hair and dodge massive spiders while navigating through the bush, with the added guarantee of pulling ticks off my body later that day. But I marched on, and eventually Louis stopped and tied his horse's reins to a tree. I caught up and looked for a place to tie my horse down, and as I was doing so tripped over a strange brown mass. I looked down and saw what Louis had wanted to show us; I was looking at a full rhino skeleton.

Femur bones, vertebrae and other bones I couldn't identify were strewn across the ground, clearly picked over by lions and leopards. But the most striking was the skull, colossal in size and eerie-looking just sitting on the ground like it was. We examined the bones, trying to figure out how they fit together. We searched for the teeth missing in the skull and found a couple that we fit back in their sockets. The brown mass I had stepped onto was the rhino's skin, dry and crumpled.

Another evening we were on a bush walk; a bush walk is exactly what it sounds like- exploring the bush on foot. Sometimes we would be learning about different trees and plants, other times searching for specific bird species. That evening we were examining tracks. We had found several lion tracks, and identified them as the lioness and her four cubs. On the walk back home we had to pass a large pond near our house. By this point the sun was setting and the sky was glowing shades of orange and red. We were walking in a disorganized line about ten feet from the water's edge when a group of six hippos suddenly popped out of the water and stood watching us. We froze, and our group leader whisper-shouted to not make any sudden movements. Apparently I had forgotten that hippos are the second most common animal to kill humans, because my jaw dropped as I marveled at the hippos' silhouette against the iconic African sunset.

And *this* is how South Africa changed me. I wrote in my piece about D.C., "there are parts of yourself you have yet to discover." My time in South Africa challenged this thought, because an experience abroad is like adding a whole other chapter to your book that you wouldn't have had otherwise. The experience never leaves you, because it imprints you. Days without running water changed me. Looking into a lion's eyes changed me. This is the greatest gift of travel: you get to carry the experience home inside of you.

I am changed because my hands have run over the skull of a rhino. I am changed because my eyes widened as those six hippos rose in them. I am changed because I felt my heart leap and my insides drop when a lioness looked at me and roared. I am changed because a silent little girl in an orphanage stole my heart.

And I hadn't even known these things were out there, I hadn't known how they would affect me. South Africa showed me this wild, extraordinary world that touched me in a way I never knew it could.

People think of Africa as a poor continent. But Africa is only poor in paper bills. Africa is so rich- rich in beauty, rich in sunsets, stories, wild thunderstorms and surprises.
--AT, February 28, 2015

SIX

The Night Before

Be prepared.

"A ship is always safe at the shore - but that is not what it is built for."
- Albert Einstein

On June 30th, 2015 I was packing my backpack, thinking about how this time the next day I would be boarding a plane to London . I figured because this was my third time leaving home this year, I wouldn't feel so extremely nervous like I felt before going to D.C. and South Africa. In many ways, my trip to London would be far easier than D.C. or South Africa. I thought that while my class at LSE would be demanding, it wouldn't be nearly as scary as learning to be an intern at Lake Research. When I left for D.C. it was my first time leaving home for an extended period of time. Before leaving for South Africa, I worried about traveling to such a drastically different place where I knew no one. I worried about making friends within the group, and I had no idea what my day-to-day life would be like there (anxiety-inducing for a Type A planner like me). London was far more welcoming in comparison. I figured it would be a city that would be somewhat similar to cities I had been to in the U.S. Several people from my group in South Africa lived in London. My best friend from home would be in London for another program at the same time, and we would be traveling together afterwards. I was comforted by the fact that I would see familiar faces there. To top it off, I would only be away for five weeks- half the time I was in both D.C. and South Africa.

Even with all this, I felt the same exact way I felt the night (and let's be honest, few days) before embarking on my last two adventures. I worried about the details: getting to my planes, packing the right things. I felt homesick even before I left home; I would start to think about all the little things I would miss like sitting on the bar stools in my kitchen while drinking coffee in the morning.

The night before I left for South Africa I felt like I was going to die. This was because I had become extremely sick from the typhoid vaccine I had to take. The vaccine was an oral pill I had to take twice a day for five days. You are supposed to do this a week before you leave (in case you do get sick), but I stupidly forgot about it until the day before I was supposed to leave. By the second day, I was practically incapacitated by the pain in my stomach. As I was doing last minute packing the night before my 5AM flight, I fainted in the bathroom as my mom and I were going over the toiletries list. I threw up, many times. At 10PM that night, my parents said there was no way I was getting on that plane the next day. (Somehow I did.)

I hope that your "night before" will not be that extreme, but I can guarantee you it will be difficult. The only advice I can give is to simply "hang in there." You will be scared because you are taking a risk. You are daring to do something different. It will be uncomfortable, it will be strange, it will be scary. But that is the trade you are making for the upcoming experience that is going to leave you a different person. You are trading those anxious moments for moments in which you will look at a landscape and feel your chest widen in amazement, or moments when you solve a problem you never would have been able to just a few weeks ago. Know that your night-before-feelings are normal, legitimate, but so worth it.

SEVEN

Mind the Gap

The London School of Economics and a Eurail Pass

metamorphosis: *noun* meta·mor·pho·sis \ ˌme-tə-ˈmȯr-fə-səsa major change in the appearance or character of someone or something - Merriam-Webster

The receptionist of Unite East Central House held open the door of my room in London as I thanked him and dragged my bags inside. The room was bare in the way all student dorms are; it had a bed, a desk and two windows. I opened the door to the bathroom, feeling immensely grateful for my own rather than a hall bathroom. I saw a shower head and curtain in the corner of the tiny room, but there was no differentiation in the floor, so when I took a shower the whole bathroom would flood. I thought of how when I checked in, a girl in front of me was complaining to the front desk about how she hadn't had hot water for three days. I said a little prayer for hot water in my room.

I looked around the room feeling a little dazed. *I guess I should unpack my bags* I thought. My parents accompanied me to D.C. and helped me settle in, and in South Africa I immediately met sixteen people upon arrival that were all sharing the same experience with me. I suddenly became overwhelmed with a pang of loneliness, then quickly pushed the thought away. I knew this feeling. Every time I arrived at a new place, I felt this fear. I reminded myself that in a couple weeks I would be leaving and wishing I could stay longer, I just had to hang in there for the beginning.

I sat down at the desk and opened the information packet I had been given. Inside was a guide to the "amenities", including how to hook up to the wifi (most important). I was a little surprised there wasn't a list of rules, and realized the stark difference between this place and my dorm in D.C. In D.C. we weren't allowed to have alcohol, to smoke, or bring any men past the lobby, which was kind of ridiculous as most people that lived there had already graduated colleges and were full-blown adults. I thought to myself, *people must have more fun here.*

Inside the packet was a paper door hanger, like the ones in hotels. One side said "Hi! Fancy a chat?" (I delighted in how British this sounded.) The guy who showed me to my room mentioned I should put this on my door to meet people. I opened my door to the hallway and looked around- no one had one on their door. Back into the folder it went.

This third portion of my gap year had been by far the hardest to plan. I had heard of the London School of Economics summer school program from my friend Ashley, (the Georgetown student who also took a gap year). When I returned home from South Africa, I became determined that this would be the final adventure of my gap year. My parents said "Great! But you have to fund it on your own."

This was daunting; the class was expensive, and I would also have to pay for housing in London for those three weeks- also pricey. In addition, one of my best friends from home was going to be in London at the exact same time, and afterwards she was planning on traveling around Europe for eleven days. It was an amazing opportunity that we were there at the same time, and I desperately wanted to join her for the traveling, but I would have to fund that on my own as well.

I was working full-time, but after doing the math several times I found I still wouldn't be able to cover the whole cost with only those paychecks. I had a free flight voucher from the contest I won, but the overall price was still steep. I knew I had one other option; I could sell my saddle. My saddle was worth a lot of money, but I did not want to let it go as it represented my riding, my passion for as long as I could remember. I debated in my head whether or not to saddle the saddle for weeks. Finally, I realized that I could either be home this summer, without friends, working a job I hated, with my saddle sitting in the garage. Or, I could let the saddle go, and go on another adventure in which I would be taking a class I was interested in, and seeing more of the world. I decided I wanted to reach for every opportunity I can possibly have- and the saddle went.

I signed up to take an international relations class titled "The Middle East in Global Politics." I have always been fascinated by the Middle East and as someone who wants to work in foreign affairs one day, I knew there is no region more complicated but important. (For those interested, LSE has classes in economics and international relations. You can take a three-week long summer course of your choosing if you have already been accepted to a university at home. Best yet, you will receive college credit for the course that you can apply to the university you plan to attend in the fall.)

I was bursting in excitement for this course, but next I had to figure out where I was going to live in London for those three weeks. LSE offered housing, but it was very expensive and most of it had filled up by the time I knew I could definitely afford to take the class. I went looking elsewhere, and found a company that rents apartments to students. It was slightly cheaper than LSE housing. I envisioned buying groceries each week and cooking in my apartment to live cheaply. Less than a week before I was supposed to leave, I found out my apartment didn't even come with bed sheets, let alone kitchen necessities like silverware, pots or plates.

After I unpacked my bags I realized my bathroom didn't even have toilet paper in it. My next task was to go grocery shopping. It would be the first time I would buy my own toilet paper.

I went downstairs and asked the man at the front desk where the nearest grocery store was, and he gave me some vague instructions that I didn't really understand. Nonetheless, I left the building and started walking. Because of my experience in D.C. I felt like I was pretty good at navigating cities. And my time in South Africa gave me this "I survived the African bush, I can do anything" mixed with "Everything's going to be ok it's all an adventure" attitude. Combined, I thought I would be able to find my way around London without a problem.

Silly, silly me. You can't just walk around a huge city and expect to find a grocery store by making turns and following streets that "look right."

I had no idea what was ahead of me.

If I learned anything in London, it was how to put myself out there. The London School of Economics had a Facebook page for students, and in the days leading up to classes starting people were organizing get-togethers over Facebook. The idea of meeting up with a random person I had never met before felt weird to me and I was wary of it. But I had decided I was going to make every effort to push myself out of my comfort zone this past year. So a few hours after my plane had landed in London, I posted on the Facebook wall.

"Just moved in today, anyone want to meet up?"

I had never done anything like that in my life. I almost wished people *wouldn't* respond. Twenty minutes later, my phone buzzed.

It was a message from a guy named Matthew from Australia.

"Hi Abby! Want to meet up tonight?"

To be honest, it scared me a little. But I agreed to meet him anyways, knowing the sooner I made connections with people the happier I would be here. I googled how to take the tube to Trafalgar Square, our meeting spot, and a few hours later I was on my way there.

I met Matthew in the iconic London spot, and he told me we were meeting others also. This was a major relief-conversation is much easier to sustain with a group than with only two people. We stood around awkwardly and asked each other the standard questions: "Where are you from?" "What are you studying in school?" "How old are you?"

Eventually we met up with the group-others from Australia, India, Italy, London and New Jersey. We ate dinner in Soho, got ice cream in Leicester Square, and ended up at Piccadilly Circus where we watched street dancers at midnight.

Throughout the night the conversation was never anything but lively, interesting, entertaining. Our backgrounds were so different that we all had a unique story to share.

Three of the people I met that night became some of my best friends during my time there: a girl from India who goes to school in Milan, a boy from India who goes to school in California, and a girl whose family lives in Switzerland and who goes to school in New Jersey. I almost didn't go meet Matthew that night. I was nervous, uncomfortable. But if I hadn't, I might never have met those people. My entire experience in London might have been different. The best things in life are the things you have to take risks for.

A few days later I was sitting in a classroom at LSE. My course consisted of a three-hour lecture and a ninety-minute discussion group each day. For the discussion element, we were divided into small groups of about ten people. The first day we introduced ourselves with our name, what country we were from, and what school we attended. There were a large amount of Americans in my class, disproportionate from the rest of the program, probably because the U.S.'s relations with the Middle East are particularly complicated. We circled around the room, and in just our small group there were several kids from Dartmouth, Yale, and Princeton. As usual, I was the only one who hadn't started college yet. I was both impressed and intimidated.

As the class discussions began, this group of Ivy-League boys proved to be particularly vocal. They were unafraid to offer their opinion, and left little room for considering whether or not they were right. They monopolized the conversation, and for the first week, I was too afraid to do anything about it.

I had never been like this before; I was always the kid in class who raised their hand and was eager to share my opinion. I had never doubted I had something worthy to say. My class in London rendered me silent. I was worried I would say something and not have all the right facts about it. I didn't want to take a stance and then have someone rip me apart, as I had seen these boys do to each other.

Each class two people had to give a ten minute long presentation summarizing the material covered in the lecture the day before. Ten minutes is a long time to be talking for, and standing up in front of this group was the absolute last thing I wanted to do. My partner and I were assigned to present on Friday of the first week on the extent of influence the United States had on the Middle East during the Cold War period. My partner and I divided up the work. I typed up my slides and emailed them to her, as she was going to put them on a PowerPoint and we planned to use her computer when presenting.

The day of our presentation, the Tube workers went on strike. No one could use the underground and the buses were running extremely slow since so many more people were having to take them. There was warning this was going to happen, so I spent the night at my friend's apartment that was in walking distance of LSE. I got to my class on time, and looked around for my partner. I watched the hands on the clock tick, and five minutes into class she still wasn't there. Not only had she done half the work, all of *my* work was on the PowerPoint on her computer.

"Just present what you can," the teacher said.

I walked up to the front of the room, shaking in fear. I nervously explained I had only done half the work, so could only present my half of the presentation. I began, but I had nothing- no slides to remind me of dates and names. I had to go entirely off of memory. I stumbled through dates of wars and treaties, and Arabic names I could barely pronounce when I *did* have them written in front of me.

But, I did it. I remembered facts, I knew names and dates and events. I shocked myself. From that day on, I found it a little easier to speak in class. I would raise my hand at least once each session, if I was sure I knew the answer. Slowly, I offered more and more.

The second week, I rubbed my temples as I stared at a computer screen in the LSE library. I looked over at my friend's screen, where she already had many pages written. It was the day before midterms, and we either had a paper to hand in or an exam to take tomorrow, so the library was packed with people studying very seriously. I was writing a paper analyzing the United States' effect on domestic politics in the Middle East during the Cold War period. To better describe my situation, I was consulting Wikipedia pages to try to figure out what I was even talking about.

Internally I was panicking a little. My friends in my class all had at least two years of college under their belts, so to them this 2000 word paper wasn't a big deal. I, on the other hand, had never written a 2000 word paper in my life. I had never written a college-level research paper. I had never even taken a college-level political science class. And this wasn't just any political science class, this was a class on the Middle East, arguably the most complicated region in the world. This wasn't just any university- this was the London School of Economics. All of these thoughts were whirling through my head, including: *why did I ever think I could do this?*

I felt overwhelmed, I felt incapable. And then I looked around at the people around me. People from all over the world, certainly the smartest young people I've ever interacted with. Next to me was my friend with whom I bonded over heated arguments about the Israel-Palestine conflicts and a weakness for Starbucks twice a day. And all of a sudden I didn't feel stressed anymore- I felt lucky.

It hit me like a wave. Here I was in the library of LSE. Around me were people who pushed me and inspired me every single day. I was uncovering a topic that has always gripped me. I thought to myself, there is nowhere I would rather be.

On the last day, we were debating whether or not the Middle East could ever have a true democracy. We asked questions like, should they even have one? Is that what they want? Is it the right, or the responsibility, of the United States to make it happen? What is democracy? Is it feasible for a democracy to provide freedoms to every single citizen? Can a democracy exist that is not secular?

I could not get enough chances to speak. I had questions, responses, defenses for everything. I had so much to say, and so much to listen to. I was unrecognizable from the mute, timid girl I was the first week. I never wanted the conversation to end.

One night, I was sitting on a couch in my friend's flat. Lounging around me was my group of friends. It was a Wednesday, so we were spending the evening at home, sharing a bottle of wine and each other's company. We were packed in her room, spread over chairs and her bed; I was sandwiched between two people on the couch. Outside the sky was darkening but her room was bright in contrast. I felt warm from the wine, lively conversation, and the bodies next to me. We talked about anything and everything- our classes, our lives back home, our mistakes in the past, our goals for the future. It was casual and normal- but big at the same time. These were big people with big plans and big potential within them. I could feel it. I basked in it.

Out of the seven of us, we came from four different countries, three different continents. At eighteen years old I was the youngest, with the rest of the group's ages ranging up to twenty-two. With some of them, the only common experience I shared was choosing to go to LSE's summer school. And yet, with this group, I felt more comfortable, more like I fit in than with any other group of people I had met before. I felt like I had finally met my tribe.

This was undoubtedly the best part about my time in London. During my high school years, I existed on the outside. I had a completely different academic experience, spending half my day at high school and the other half at college classes.

Instead of participating in a school sport, I had my horseback riding. This was intentional, but it was difficult. It was the path I chose, but it was a lonely one.

Since I moved to Vermont at age twelve, I had a hard time finding "my kind" of people. Everyone knows what I'm talking about- people that care about the same things you do, that have similar aspirations, or maybe obstacles. People that you can completely be yourself around. I made a few close connections like this in Vermont, but for the most part, I always felt like I was on a different page than the people around me.

In London, I could discuss the U.S.'s foreign policy towards the Middle East, and people would not only listen- they would push back. They would be talking about a religion I knew nothing about, and then teach me. I was in awe of their accomplishments, future plans, and stories.

At night the club is dark and my friend's faces flash among the neon lights. Bodies move to my right, to my left, in front of and behind me. The music blares and I feel it beating inside my chest. A popular song comes on, and suddenly everyone is hit was a fresh shot of energy. People jump and drop low in sync, arms go up in the air. I catch my friend's eye, and he takes my hands in his and twirls me. We all dance in a circle around each other, we are unburdened and unapologetic.

These are the same people I sit next to in class, the same people I crammed for a final exam with. These are the same people I would share a dinner table with. I will always treasure the relationships I had in London, because they reminded that there are people out there that I can feel connected to. I had forgotten what it was like to feel a complete sense of belonging. Now I know it is there, I know I will always look for it, and I know to never settle for anything less.

While I was taking a class at LSE, one of my closest friends from home was in London with a study abroad program associated with her university. Our programs finished around the same time, which seemed so serendipitous we decided to explore the continent more together afterwards. Her class ended two days before mine, so she planned to go to Amsterdam for two days, and we would meet in Paris. I landed in Paris at 10am on a Saturday and she would be taking a train there that same day. As I was exiting the plane, it hit me that I did not have a plan for how I would find the hostel. I had the address, but my phone did not have cellular data, so I couldn't use Google maps or anything like that to search how to get there. I would have to use a map, and I was a bit stumped by how *primitive* that seemed. I immediately texted my friend (also named Abby) to see how she was planning to get there.

After forty-five minutes of searching for an ATM, figuring out how to exchange my currency, looking at a map to find a bus, then a train, to get me to the hostel, buying a bus ticket, and asking questions in the limited French I had, I finally walked out to the bus stop. The weight of my backpack was beginning to take a toll on me. I still had no response from Abby.

I sat on the bus and eavesdropped on the French conversations going on around me, trying to pick out words I recognized. Eventually the bus stopped. I had no idea if this was my stop or not, but when everyone got off the bus I figured I should too. We had arrived at a train station. I thought I was doing pretty well; I knew what station I had to get to eventually. After brief confusion about how to buy a ticket and more broken French, I looked at another map and found which train line I needed to take.

When I got onto the train, I had another predicament. My backpack was too big for both it and me to sit on the seat, but if I put it at my feet it blocked the way. The only option, besides standing, was to put it in a seat next to me, thus taking up two seats. I knew this wasn't really acceptable, but I couldn't imagine standing with it. Its enormous weight was causing my back to ache and I was sweating. In a wave of frustration I flung the backpack into the seat next to me, ignoring the dirty looks from other passengers. Still no response from Abby.

After spending a half hour on the train, I finally arrived at the stop I believed would be closest to my hostel. I emerged onto the Parisian street and realized I now had no clue how to get from this train station to the hostel. I looked around for a map and couldn't find one. All I had was a street name: no smartphone, no map, and no one to accompany me. Not knowing what else to do, I started to walk around, hoping I might see the street I was looking for. After doing this for about twenty minutes I was getting nowhere. The weight of my backpack was rubbing the skin on my shoulders raw. A young guy, noticing how lost I looked, came up to me and started speaking. Being lost in a foreign city was already making me feel nervous, I was too scared to talk to this guy. After not responding to him, he grabbed my arm.

"*Mademoiselle, es-tu perdu? Tu es très jolie!*"

I did not want him to know I was lost. I decided I couldn't wander the streets any longer. I looked for a shop and found one with a woman inside. I nervously walked up to her and asked in the best French I could muster if she knew where this street was. She didn't. My heart sunk and I turned to walk away. But then, she pulled out her iPhone, and began looking it up for me. She found the street and gave me directions, in French that I (mostly) understood. So grateful, I set off in the direction she had pointed me in.

At this point my phone buzzed. My heart leapt, and I prayed it was Abby informing me she had arrived in Paris. I looked at the screen and saw it was a text from Abby's mother. *This is strange,* I thought.

The text read: "Abby lost her phone and missed her train leaving Amsterdam. Not sure when she'll be arriving in Paris. Please let me know when you meet up with her."

In that instant, I wanted to sit down on the sidewalk and start crying. Here I was in a foreign city, totally lost and alone, with no idea when or how I would be meeting up with Abby who was supposed to be my travel partner. I wanted to turn around, go back to the airport, buy a ticket to London and reunite with my friends still there that I already missed terribly. I took a deep breath and decided I had to focus solely on getting to my hostel. After walking another half hour, I finally found it. When I arrived at the beautiful, so typically European-looking building that had the name and address I recognized, I almost cried in relief.

I checked into the hostel and immediately took a shower to make myself feel better. But I was so concerned about where Abby was- my worst fear would be she wouldn't be able to get to Paris that night. I didn't want to spend my first night in a hostel alone, but I began to mentally prepare myself for the possibility of having to.

The entire day went by without hearing any more from her. I explored the streets, had lunch at a cafe, and went into Printemps, all things I planned to do with her. Nonetheless, the minute I got onto the Parisian streets I felt instantly better. The architecture was beautiful, the people were lively, the early evening air was warm. I finally returned to my hostel as it began to get dark.

At ten o-clock that night, my phone beeped. It was a Facebook message from Abby that read- "Just arrived at Paris train station. I'm ten minutes walking distance from hostel."

The first thing I felt was immense relief. Secondly, I feel concerned she was going to be walking at night alone. I didn't know how she had been able to Facebook message me, because she didn't have a phone. But I didn't care, I was so excited to see my friend's face, the next ten minutes I waited anxiously. Ten minutes, then thirty, then almost an hour had passed. Abby still hadn't arrived at the hostel, and I had no way of contacting her.

At eleven o'clock I got a message from Abby that she was in the lobby of the hostel. I flew out of the room, sprinted down the stairs, and tackled her in an embrace. She was tearing up- from the exhaustion, frustration and probably fear from her day.

The closest restaurant still open was a pizza place across the street, and we were both so hungry we didn't look any further. Over slices of pizza Abby described to me how she had lost her phone, missed her train and therefore had to take five different trains to get to Paris, arriving at Paris and, after getting lost also, got directions from strangers who allowed her to use their phone to message me. But these people had also tried to get her to go somewhere with them, and that is why it took her so long to get to the hostel.

The day was traumatic for both of us. But now here we were: eating pizza in a little restaurant, lit up against the night, on a quaint side street in Paris. I felt so comforted to finally have my friend there. But I also felt that after that day, we both could overcome anything. It made my first day of college feel like a piece of cake.

Thinking about the twelve days I spent traveling in Europe: it was the little moments that mattered, that will stay with me.

When our train first pulled into Interlaken, Switzerland, Abby and I squeezed close together to gape at the jaw-dropping view outside the window. Interlaken means "between lakes," but this was like no lake I had ever seen before. The water had a magnificent teal color, framed by bright green and blue mountains. We got off the train dazed by this small pocket of beauty we had just arrived in. Interlaken is a small town with a few quaint streets with restaurants, chocolatiers and shops that sell Swiss army knives. There are a few buses, and we arrived with a vague idea of how to get to the hostel we were staying at. We looked around, and didn't see anywhere to buy a bus ticket. We walked up to the bus driver and asked him where to buy tickets. He responded in a language we couldn't even identify. Not knowing what else to do, we showed him our Eurail passes, hoping they would count for something. To our luck, he waved us onto the bus. Confused but grateful we took a seat, again not sure what stop we were getting off at. We hoped we would just recognize our hostel, and that ended up working out for us.

In Interlaken we were staying in a hostel known as the "Tent Village." The Tent Village was a compound of little, yellow and white striped tents surrounded by incredible mountain ranges on all sides. The days were overcast and the clouds would hang below the mountain peaks. The Tent Village was slightly outside the town. Across from the Tent Village was a grocery store, and behind that was a flat field that stretched for miles until reaching the base of another mountain. One evening Abby and I decided to explore. We started out on the path, where we passed nothing but several dilapidated barns. A girl riding a horse passed us, her Jack Russell terrier running alongside them. An intense longing for horses hit us both, riding being the sport that bonded us in the first place. The lush field stretched on every side of us, framed by the snowy-peaked mountain ranges that encircled us. I felt like we were on a different planet. Even though we are from Vermont, a rural, mountainous area also, this felt different. The emptiness was eerie but comforting at the same time. We were the only two people in this beautiful, hidden corner of the world. Since I was twelve years old Abby and I traveled to horse shows together, and our favorite activity in our free time was to "explore" the area we were in. Usually this just meant walking around outside whatever Hampton Inn we were staying at. Now here we were, discovering a whole other continent together. The broadness of the world hit me in that very moment.

When you are so far from everything that defines you-your family, your school, your hometown, your activities- who are you? The only thing that defines you is your spirit for adventure you are satisfying. This makes you feel both empty and full at the same time. You forget who you are for a moment, because you are adapting, breaking down, building up- transforming into a more complete version of yourself. I was trying to comprehend all these things in that moment on that path in Interlaken.

In front of the Tent Village was a miniature mountain bike course, with little hills and jumps people would ride over. During our time there we met and befriended two guys who were med students in Canada. Late one night I was brushing my teeth in the bathroom, getting ready to go to bed. One of the guys, named John, came in to brush his teeth too. As we were talking, out of the blue he asked me, "Do you want to go explore?" The place was kind of mysterious.

"Okay" I agreed.

We walked around the edge of the compound until we got to the main road. This was the "busiest" road in Interlaken, which meant every once in a while you saw a car pass. There were no street lights but the brightness of the stars provided light. I looked down the road, where it twisted in-between two mountains. To our right was the miniature mountain bike course. All of a sudden John took my hand and took off running toward to dirt course. I was confused, but I ran after him anyways. He held my hand and jumped over the ridges, ran up and down the hills, leading me. I'm not sure why he did this, but I think the idea just struck him and he acted. Eventually he stopped, and we looked at each other and smiled at the ridiculousness of it.

A week later, Abby and I were sitting on the beach on our last night in Nice. We faced the dark sea, a bottle of grapefruit-flavored wine wedged into the rocks between us. We had swiped two glasses from our hostel, and sipped on the sweet flavored wine, savoring our last few days before having to return home. To our right and left the coastline stretched, lit up by the lights of restaurants and shops. To me the Mediterranean looked intimidating at night, but there were several people still swimming. I didn't want to talk about the fact this was our last night, so instead we talked about the future: what we would be doing next summer, when we graduated, in ten years.

Suddenly someone grabbed my shoulders from behind. I practically jumped to my feet, confused as the only person I knew here was Abby, and she was sitting to my right. I turned around, and it was John. I knew that he and his travel partner were going to be in Nice at the same time as us, but I have no idea how they found us on that beach that night. They sat down on either side of us and we recounted our last few days to each other. We had been in Milan, they had been in Geneva. We laughed about my gambling experience at Monte Carlo, they told us about forgetting about what day they were supposed to leave Switzerland and having to run to the train station panicked. Even though we had spent barely two days with each other in Interlaken, it felt like we were reconnecting with old friends. When they said goodbye, it struck me that I would probably never see them again.

In Milan, we stayed at an Airbnb, meaning we essentially rented an apartment for the two nights we were there, as opposed to staying in a hostel. When we first got there, we were so excited to see our apartment had a balcony. It was a tiny space with two wobbly chairs that overlooked the parking lot- nothing scenic. But we cherished that balcony. Each night we would walk to the grocery store down the street, and buy a bottle of Chardonnay that cost two euros. We were extremely wary of this two-euro wine at first, but we were on a budget so the price was ideal. To our surprise it tasted fantastic (or we just have no taste in wine, this is a more likely explanation). Along with the wine we bought a bag of peanuts. We would pour the wine into stemmed glasses, and the peanuts into baby-blue china bowl that happened to come with the apartment and remark on how classy we were. We brought the wine glasses, the bowl of peanuts and a deck of cards onto the balcony. It would already be dark out, so we would leave the door open to give us enough light to play gin-rummy. Since I am normally very competitive, Abby would only play cards with me when I was drinking wine. Magically I would drop the tense edge I bring to every game, no matter how trivial.

The stairs to the main subway station in Milan are right next to the Duomo Cathedral. The first time I saw the Duomo, my jaw physically dropped. I had never seen anything like it. The white walls were covered in intricate designs, drawings and script. It had peaks that poke into the sky, giving it a castle-like image. You could stare at it forever, and continue to notice new things. I had a harder time saying goodbye to the Duomo than just about anything else in Europe. The last night, I lingered before walking down the stairs to the subway, not wanting to leave its grey walls striking against the dark sky. Outside there was a street performer singing opera music in a deep, rich voice. I was so enchanted I had to pause at the top of the staircase, trying desperately to commit the moment to memory.

These were the magical moments. This is the gift of traveling; you experience these things that seem like only a small part of the experience, but they turn out to be the most significant. Our parking-lot balcony was significant, the lonely path in Interlaken was significant, the two-euro wine was significant. These are the things that leave you more open, more knowing, humbler. These were the big things.

Near the end of my time in South Africa, my group and I traveled to Mozambique to spend three nights and days on the beach. It was supposed to be a sort of "break" from or "reward" for the intense volunteer work we were doing in the bush and in the community. It turned out our volunteer work was not so intense, but of course we carried on to Mozambique anyways. In the days leading up to our departure, the whole house was buzzing in excitement. Everyone was ecstatic about the idea of relaxing on the beach, seeing the ocean, and just getting a change of scenery. But there was a part of me that was uneasy. I didn't feel like I had earned this, and that upset me.

When we got there, we arrived at a beautiful stretch of beach we had all to ourselves. The ocean was a deep blue and had waves like I'd never seen before. My next three days would consist of tanning, swimming, and drinking cocktails on the beach- sounds like paradise right? But in the beginning I continued to struggle with the feeling that I didn't deserve this.

I thought about my family back home in the freezing Vermont winter- and felt much guilt over where I was. *Why did I get to be here, while they were there?* Eventually I gave myself an attitude intervention and told myself there was no sense in not enjoying the trip because of this feeling- and it worked. But in the beginning I truly believed this experience was one I did not deserve.

This feeling came back before I left for London. In the weeks leading up to my departure I thought, why should I get to go explore Europe, as opposed to my family, or my coworkers at the deli? As I sat in the airport waiting to board the plane, I had the worst feeling that I was not meant to be doing this. I looked around at all the other passengers, and everyone had someone accompanying them. I watched a young girl with her two parents, and felt incredibly jealous for a moment, that she had these two people taking care of her. I knew it was ridiculous, I wanted to be independent, I certainly did not want my parents joining me in London. But I felt like again, I was alone. That feeling coupled with an unexplainable feeling of guilt for the opportunities I've had.

Five weeks later I was sitting on a rock with the waves of the Mediterranean Sea splashing just before my feet. I squinted at the blinding-blue sky, feeling the sun tan my skin. Sitting there, I was hit by this thought that surprised me: I did not feel guilty. In the last five weeks I had traveled to five different countries; I had eaten incredible meals, seen spectacular views, visited some of the world's greatest museums. And for the first time in my life I thought, *it is ok I have had these opportunities.*

Before, I could create practical reasons for why I deserved to take the class to LSE. I told myself, I was making an effort to understand a region that needs the world's help. I figured I am going to have a career relating to this subject one day, this was just the beginning of the background knowledge I need to make a difference in the world one day. To top it off, I was getting credit for the class too. But what I finally accepted on that rock in Nice, is that an experience doesn't have to have a "practical" justification to be of worth. It is important enough to see a new place, to try a new food, to meet new people. There is worth in simply sipping coffee in a cafe in a foreign country and people-watching. There was also worth in sitting on that rock, gazing into the sea, letting my mind be blown by the beauty of my surroundings. Moments like this make you more appreciative, they let you truly feel what is and what is not important, they ignite a drive in you. I did not feel guilt. I felt happy.

When I was in Europe and I would call my family and friends back home I would tell them, "I am so happy here." It was the first time in my life I had pronounced happiness so honestly, openly and willingly. This is not to say I had never felt happy before, but it was sometimes burdened by other emotions, particularly the feeling that I did not deserve this happiness.

Before my gap year, I was unhappy in several ways. My family's move to Vermont when I was twelve years old uprooted my life and I never really fully recovered (to my own fault partially.) I couldn't let go of the loss of my best friends from Chicago being in my daily life. I was never satisfied with my school experience compared to the curriculum in Chicago I thrived in. I was bitter, and this bitterness prevented me from ever accepting Vermont and so I focused my energy in finding an endless list of things I did not like about it. My parents divorced- never a pleasant process. And while riding was what kept me going, it simultaneously brought strain and disappointment.

In hindsight, my gap year was a road to a happier version of myself. My time in D.C. was challenging, but moments of happiness peeked out there. In South Africa there were certainly moments where I was truly, unmatchably happy. During my time there, I got to be carefree in a way I had never been able to before. I felt like we were living in this parallel universe: just me and my teammates, in the African bush, with these magnificent animals, with little we had to do or be responsible for. My mom saw pictures of me and said "You look happy. Are you happy?" When I came home my friends told me I seemed more relaxed, I seemed happier. Still, I could not offer the declaration myself yet. I was closer, but it still had to be pointed out to me.

But in London, I knew. It would hit me when I was out to dinner with friends; it would hit me sitting in class. I felt undeniably happy, in a simpler way than I had ever felt happiness before. This change within me is the greatest gift an experience has ever given me; greater than a line on my resume, greater than any paycheck, any wild story to tell. But it wasn't just a gift, it was something I worked for, even when I didn't know I was working for it. It is something I took risks for. It is something I will try my hardest to hold on to.

WHO I AM NOW

My pre-gap year life was centered around one thing and one thing only: horses. Every moment I wasn't in school, I was in the saddle...or mucking a stall, or brushing a horse, or setting jumps, then asking again if there were any more horses that needed to be ridden, repeat. The minute I was out of class I was on my way to the barn. I would go to my high school classes in the morning, ride in the middle of the day, then go to my college classes at UVM in the late afternoon/evening. If there were extra horses that needed to be worked, I would go back to the barn for a second time that day. On Saturdays and Sundays I was there at 7AM to feed the horses their breakfast, even on Vermont winter mornings so cold my fingers would go numb within minutes. I remember kneeling outside, scraping the ice out of the horses' water buckets, my fingers screaming for a break from the arctic temperature. Even on Mondays when the barn was closed, I couldn't resist but stop by to visit my horse, to take him out for grass, brush the shavings out of his tail, tend to him like my child.

All my excess time, money, and energy was spent on riding. However even though I was happiest at the barn, riding took a major toll on me at the same time. My family didn't have the limitless resources the sport requires. I was so fortunate my family was willing to pour everything we had into it, but sometimes it wasn't enough. This was a difficult pill to swallow. Then there is the unbelievable fragility of these animals. I saw so many horses I loved get injured and have an entire season or even career be forever changed by a lengthy, painful, and expensive recovery. I saw one of my own horses, who tried his heart out for me every day, break his leg in front of me and have to be put down an hour later. I watched my best friend rehabilitate her horse for over a year, only to have him never recover. I saw my trainer's life be changed when she was thrown from a horse and shattered her femur. Horses broke my heart, more than once.

But in the end, the partnership I had with my horse was the most important relationship in my life. I know I am the person I am today because of riding; it made me strong, independent, and persistent. Pre-gap year, I didn't think there was anything that could make as happy as I was when riding a horse. I deeply feared what my life would look like without it, and internalized this fear because I truly did not believe anything could fulfill me in the same way. Horses were not only my "everything," I thought of them as the only thing.

But here I am, almost a full year later, and I am okay. I am more than okay; I am sitting on a Eurail train on my way to Switzerland, and I am the happiest I have ever been. Horses will always be a part of me, and I have no doubt I will find my way back to them. But now, I have this desire to experience the world that I never could have known when the barn was my entire world.

One night I was at a club in London with a group of friends, and we were dancing. The loud music energized me as I sang along to the lyrics, and we jumped and danced around each other because we were young and free and happy. At one point a girl about eight years older than me looked at me and asked, "How old are you again?"

"18!" I shouted over the Drake song.

"How amazing it is, to be eighteen and have your whole life ahead of you!" she smiled, throwing her hands up in the air.

The exchange struck me as so random, but so true that I stopped dancing. I stood there for just a second, beaming. I won't ever forget that moment, as it stirred something inside of me. In my gap year, I've made connections with people who are so different, but who shared their hearts with me and I did in return. My mind was stretched, my opinion was challenged, and I've soaked up more knowledge I ever knew I could. It took time without horses to see I had all those moments ahead of me.

I hate saying goodbye. My natural instinct is to simply evade situations I don't like, so I would rather say "see you later" and pretend I'm seeing the person the next day. I had to say goodbye many times this past year, to people that had become incredibly important to me.

My first difficult goodbye occurred on the DC metro. Allegra was my fellow intern and became a close friend during my time in DC. Being six years older than me, she took me "under her wing" and I'm so grateful for it. Moving to a city on my own at age 17 was more than a little terrifying, and working at LRP was even more terrifying (in the beginning). With Allegra, I felt immediately I had someone to ask questions, share a work load, and confide in. We rode the metro home to the same stop together each night, and each time we would separate to walk home she was say "text me when you get home safe!" This meant a lot to me, because even as I was very independent there, it felt so good to feel like there was someone looking after me.

Then there was Ashley, my friend from Georgetown to whom I credit for completely changing the way I felt about starting college, in a good way. Being with her, I saw how magical the college experience is- learning about what is important to you and having the freedom to figure out who you are. It made me genuinely excited for college in a way I never was before. I said goodbye to her on M Street in Georgetown, and as she walked away she turned around and shouted back at me, "Abby, I'm glad you came!"

I thought about how scared I was the first two weeks, when I begged my parents to let me come home, almost choosing to quit.

"I'm glad I came too," I shouted back, completely meaning it.

My entire last week in South Africa, I was dreading that goodbye. The group of people I was with had been my companions every day, all day, for ten whole weeks. We ate meals together, did every activity together, slept under the same roof. We made each other laugh; we solved problems only having each other to figure it out. We faced days without running water together. We danced all night in the warm South African air together. And we never saw anyone else. This kind of experience makes people dependent on one other in a way you don't even realize in the present moment.

We traveled to the airport together, but my plane left an hour earlier than theirs, as I was flying to New York and they were going to London. When it was time, I hugged each person goodbye, sadly but composed. As soon as I passed through security on my own and took a seat waiting to board my plan, I burst into tears. It was inconceivable that the people that had been by my side for the past ten weeks were suddenly gone. It felt unnatural, like a gaping hole was left next to me.

Even though I've had some practice now with goodbyes, I'd still rather think of it as a "see you later." And sometimes that turns out to be true; I saw several of my friends from South Africa in London and I reunited with one of them in Boston when she was visiting America. Seeing them in such a different setting was surreal. I remembered them dressed in safari pants, hair tangled as we trekked through the bush searching for snares. We reunited in dresses, mascara and dress shirts on the bustling streets of London.

You may say goodbye, but you never know when another's path will cross with your own again. I firmly believe the people you make connections with along the way were meant to be in your life for a reason. Your relationships have a purpose with a relevance to that time period of your life. Some will lead you to revelations about your own self, some to realizations about the world around you. Sometimes, you are lucky to meet someone who is going to teach you something, someone who is older and wiser and is willing to share what they've picked up along the way. Sometimes a relationship forces you to step up and lead-to be the knowing one yourself-and that is a blessing too.

I was lucky to meet so many girls in my gap year that made me think "She is so cool. (Or so smart, or so brave.) I want to be just like her one day." I now have not one but many girls I consider to be my role models, a global sisterhood I can call on for advice, share ideas with, and confide in.

I remember walking to class with one of these girls in London. As we walked we debated the Israel-Palestine conflict, she leaning pro-Israel and me slightly pro-Palestine. I felt intimidated at first as I wanted to articulate my opinion intelligently, knowing this was a sensitive topic, and I was just getting to know her. She told anecdotes and recited facts that pushed me to question what I thought, but forced me to stand by my perspective. We raised our voices and we did not agree. I was relishing this, there is nothing I love more than a thought-provoking conversation. But afterwards, I started to worry.

Had I just offended this girl I wanted to become friends with? Will she not want to be my friend because we have different opinions on such a divisive topic?

We neared our classroom and she said something along the lines of "I love having conversations like this and talking to people who will disagree with me." I almost smiled in relief.

I take comfort in the fact that if it is hard to say goodbye, that means something. As heart-wrenching as they are, I know I am fortunate to have had many goodbyes this past year that left me with a squeeze in my chest and tears swelling behind my eyes. Hard goodbyes mean that person has touched you. I will try my best to turn all my "goodbye's" into "see you later's."

There is a quote that states, "Life isn't about finding yourself. Life is about creating yourself." I like this quote; I have it in my room, painted on a wooden board that I was given as a graduation gift. But this quote is not entirely true. In life, you will "find yourself" in places or moments that you did not create yourself.

I first "found myself" on the back of a horse, and it was not me but God, or whatever higher power you believe in, that created that animal. I then found myself in Washington, D.C., a city created not by me, but by visionaries and leaders before me. I found myself again in the beauty of South Africa and the sacredness of the wildlife there that I felt connected to. I found myself in a classroom in London. I have found myself in the souls of people that I felt challenged, loved or inspired by. And those moments, when you find yourself in something, are of immense worth.

Now I am about to start the next chapter of my life at Wake Forest University. It is the final plane I will board this year, this time without a return ticket. I am a different person boarding that plane than I would have been had I not taken a gap year. I am wiser, stronger. I know more, I've seen more, and I want more. The world is so much bigger and grander than I knew it to be, and I hope your world will be changed by your gap year. So take that leap of faith- go see what ignites you, discover what drives you, find what enrages you, learn how to change it. The world needs more people who are curious, open and inspired. Take a gap year and become the person you want to be, or the person you never knew you could become.